W9-BIE-311

Become a

PUBLISHED
AUTHOR

Foreword by DAN POYNTER

∞INFINITY
PUBLISHING

Copyright © 2012 by Infinity Publishing

All rights reserved. No part of this book shall be reproduced or transmitted in any form or by any means, electronic, mechanical, magnetic, photographic including photocopying, recording or by any information storage and retrieval system, without prior written permission of the publisher. No patent liability is assumed with respect to the use of the information contained herein. Although every precaution has been taken in the preparation of this book, the publisher and author assume no responsibility for errors or omissions. Neither is Infinity Publishing responsible for any policy changes such as those that occur from time to time and are a necessary part of the evolution of our service. Neither is any liability assumed for damages resulting from the use of the information contained herein. Note that this material is subject to change without notice.

ISBN 978-0-7414-1000-9

Published by:

INFINITY PUBLISHING

1094 New DeHaven Street, Suite 100
West Conshohocken, PA 19428-2713

Info@InfinityPublishing.com
www.BuyBooksOnTheWeb.com
www.InfinityPublishing.com
Toll-free (877) BUY-BOOK
Local Phone (610) 941-9999
Fax (610) 941-9959

91 Main Street
Concord, MA 01742
(978) 371-9102

Printed in the United States of America
Published June 2012

Version 4.41

For all of the people and aspiring writers who have dreamed
of writing and publishing a book

. . . and to the authors we have had the honor to help
tell their stories to the world.

Table of Contents

Foreword

Imagine your thrill of accomplishment when you receive proof copies of your soon-to-be-published book in the mail. Bask in the glow of satisfaction from people approaching you at a conference with a copy of your book for you to autograph. Think about the personal achievement when you're interviewed for an article based on your book. Imagine the public acclaim that comes with being a published author.

Your published book provides more credibility than anything else does because the power of the printed word is omnipotent. Throughout history, people have always placed a higher value on books than any other form of communication. This is why authors are so highly valued in our society.

People want to believe that if you invested the time to write a book, you must know something of value. Most likely you probably do. You know the content of your book better than anyone else: after all, you did the necessary research and pulled it all together with your unique personal experiences. You've honed your writing to reach a specific audience interested in learning more about the topic you're an expert on. Your published book brings more credibility to whatever you are writing about. Your authored book makes you an authority!

Successful novelists are masterful storytellers who skillfully tailor their plots into compelling and entertaining books. Everyone enjoys sharing a good story—when your book is published, the novel they're talking about could be the one you wrote. Nothing is more memorable than a well-told story.

There are many reasons for authoring a book. Some people seek fame and fortune, and some other folks simply have a personal mission to be expressive through their published words. The shared commonality of all authors is they love the creative challenge of connecting with readers benefiting from the author's applied wordsmithing skills.

In this brave new world of book publishing, every writer has the opportunity to take the leap of faith to publish his or her book and make it available for public consumption. Now is the time to finish writing the book you have been thinking about or working on and take the first giant step to becoming a published author. This book will explain exactly how to do it.

— Dan Poynter, author of *Self-Publishing Manual*

Introduction

Welcome to Infinity Publishing. And let me say what an amazing time in our world's history it is for you to become a published author!

There's an old saying "you are what you read." I believe it may be more appropriate to say you are what you write! If you're like many newly minted authors, your book, when it's finished, will energize you and most probably change your life and the lives of others, as your book becomes a permanent addition to the knowledge tree of original authored works.

This is the age of the author, a new era where people like you and millions of aspiring writers and authors can publish without limits—whether you have a personal need to leave your "life mark" on the universe, a professional need to publish a "book of expertise" to attract more customers, or the desire to finally put to use your classical training as a writer to launch a "masterpiece of fiction" to the masses. For people of all ages and cultures, the idea of someday writing a book has now become a reality. And it's happening with speed, as countless new titles are being published, reviewed, and purchased by readers around the world. The Internet has brought the world to your fingertips where you can write, publish, and market your book from wherever you are with a computer and a connection to the digital cloud.

Advancements in print-on-demand, online distribution, eBook reading devices, and the way we socialize online with services like Facebook and Twitter have forever changed the way we think about books—where we buy them, how we read them, and how they get published. In this New Book, New World of Publishing, the opportunity for you to tell your story and do it credibly and affordably has never been more compelling. With a publishing partner to support you and a global marketplace of buyers, you need only be the most relevant to your reader to achieve success as a published author.

Relevance is king in today's world of keyword search *algorithms* from the likes of Google and Amazon and other search engines and online bookstores. Think of it as a continuing process of matching the thoughts and actions of your reader with the content in and around your book. From the embryonic stage of idea creation, to the moment a reader begins searching for your book or topic of interest, relevance is a factor. The good news is that you can now design and create a relevant foundation for your book that includes a unique cover design, title, and all types of content related to your book, whether in print, audio, or eBook.

Mixed-media books are the future and you as an author can now affordably offer your book to readers in the format they prefer. Some people are always on the go and only have time for car audio, others prefer digital eBooks that they can carry wherever they are, and for the majority of readers, providing a quality hardbound or softcover book will continue to satisfy their needs. New capabilities that include video and other device-driven features are here, and there are more on the way. Readers have preferences, and just as we have our favorite restaurants, each of your readers has his or her preferred reading format and place to purchase books.

Bookstores are near and dear to many of us who write and read books. They along with other brick-and- mortar stores will still be with us, but the acceptance and growth of online bookstores is staggering, and we are only at the tip of the iceberg! Book buyers around the globe are now in control—they may see your book in the review section of a magazine, but more than likely they will be searching for a specific topic of interest, reading a blog, or seeing an article online that will spark their discovery of your book.

Many of these new storefronts are connected to specialized niche content that will interest a very targeted group of readers.

These smaller markets, or niches, are often overlooked by the old-guard publishers because of their size, as they need a larger number of buyers to recover their costs. The New Book, New World of Publishing has created an immense opportunity for books from infinite origins, no matter the size, as the cost of publishing and marketing to these smaller audiences has been reduced. Additionally, writing shorter books on very broadly appealing topics is an opportunity in the new publishing revolution, as readers are looking for ways to learn and be entertained in smaller slices of time.

Marketing your book in this new publishing landscape has developed into an incredible opportunity for you and those who are motivated and ready to embrace technology and the Internet. Creating relationships, partnerships, and communicating your message on a global scale can now be achieved without ever leaving your favorite chair. By combining traditional marketing strategies and the power of the "Net," the globe is your playing field where only the amount of time in a day may limit what you can achieve.

It is my hope that you are as excited as we are about the future of publishing. You are at the beginning of a journey at a time when you literally have the world by your fingertips. Focus on what you love and pick a publishing partner you can trust to help you to do the rest. We welcome the opportunity to earn your trust in this New Book, New World of Publishing.

Sincerely,

Infinity Publishing

Part 1

PUBLISHING
WITH
INFINITY

In the ever-changing world of book publishing, selecting the best publisher for your book is the most important decision you will make in determining the successful future of your book. We want you to understand the important author-friendly advantages that you will benefit from as an Infinity author.

When you publish your book with Infinity, you are granting us permission to publish and distribute your book in exchange for royalties paid monthly, on each book sold. Infinity is identified by the assigned ISBN as the publisher of record and is listed as such in Bowker's Books In Print. You, the author, retain all rights; however, by entering into our publishing agreement and paying a one-time setup fee, you are authorizing Infinity to be the publisher of your book, which enables us to make your print, eBook, or audio book available for sale to the public through our far-reaching global channels of distribution. You will have the peace of mind of knowing your book will never go out of print.

Infinity differs from the more traditional mainstream publishing houses in ways that clearly benefit our authors. This part of our guidebook explains each of these major areas of positive differences and why our publishing model is a good match for your soon-to-be-published book.

The Infinity Difference

Freedom of expression

Suppose you had received an advance from a mainstream publisher for the exclusive right to publish your book. The publisher would then own the content and be free to edit or modify it without your consent. In mainstream publishing, the publisher's vision of the book's content always prevails.

At Infinity, you own all rights, hold the Library of Congress copyright, and have complete editorial control over the content of your book. We want authors to retain all rights to their content. We recognize that, as the author, you are far more familiar with the content and the target market you wrote your book for than we could ever hope to be. Our experience has shown that when authors own the content they are more motivated to make good things happen with their books.

Open access to publish and promote your work

We don't require your book to be submitted to us by an agent, and we have no gatekeepers making arbitrary judgments about the marketability of your book. We won't lie to you either; we won't try to seduce you into publishing with us by proclaiming your book will sell thousands of copies—no one can project the future sales of a book.

We do openly acknowledge the fact that the success of every book we publish depends entirely on the merits of the book and the promotional efforts of the author—with the many changing facets of the publishing industry, this fact, regarding the merits of the book and the proactive involvement of the author to promote the book, is increasingly true of all publishers. Since Infinity's start of business in 1997, our continuing mission is to provide a publishing and distribution platform—second to none—that's readily accessible for all authors to publish almost any book, and we are supportive of our authors' efforts to promote their books.

The opportunity to profit from your work

Infinity profits as you do—from the sale of books. It is our firm belief that our authors deserve a large share of the profit when their books sell, and the opportunity to earn higher royalties for the life of a book that never goes out of print.

Traditionally published authors start to earn royalties only after their book has sold in sufficient numbers to earn out the advance paid, and with the high percentage of books that don't sell enough copies to cover the advance, many authors never see a penny in royalties. As an Infinity author, you are paid royalties on your first book sold providing you with the immediate opportunity to begin recouping your publishing investment.

Traditional publishers pay royalties quarterly due to their need to manage their cumbersome return policy for bookstores. As an Infinity author, you will often enjoy a higher royalty rate on books sold, and royalties will be reported to you on a monthly basis.

Infinity's value-added pricing enables authors of nonfiction books, and novelists with an established following of readers, to increase the retail price above the suggested retail price, which is based on competitive pricing of softcover trade books. When it comes to pricing, we are guided by the author's knowledge of his or her target market and the cover price of similar mainstream books on the topic.

A non-exclusive publishing agreement

As an Infinity author, you have the freedom to publish anywhere you please. If you get a better offer or if you become unhappy with Infinity for any reason, or no reason, you are free to leave without a hassle. Authors publish with Infinity under a non-exclusive publishing agreement that allows the author to withdraw from this author-friendly arrangement at any time. Upon written notice of cancellation by the author, the book can be removed from our unique book-publishing system in a matter of a week.

We place no encumbrances on your book, as other nontraditional publishers might try to do. The rights to the traditionally published book will only revert back to you upon your written request, and then, only after the publisher declares the book officially "out of print." Infinity publishes books at the pleasure of and by the authorization of our authors. We don't "fence in" our authors; thus, we have a vested interest in keeping them happy with our unequaled style of publishing and customer service. Unlike traditional houses, we don't tie up the rights to your next book with a first right of refusal. When you're ready to publish your next book, we trust the outstanding service you've received will make Infinity your obvious choice.

An author-friendly environment

After more than a decade of open communications with our authors, Infinity has earned an exceptional reputation in the industry for setting the "Gold Standard" for customer service. Our publishing model is transparent and our contact with our authors is continuous. Real, live people located here in the United States answer the phone when authors call in to ask questions or place book orders. E-mails are welcomed and we do our best to reply in a timely manner—though at times we may need to do a bit of research to provide correct and definitive answers. Infinity's *Author's Advocate* newsletter is our official monthly connection with our authors; this is how we keep you abreast of what's what, what's happening, and what's hot for promoting books.

We blog, Facebook, Twitter, and post relevant updated information at www.InfinityPublishing.com and www.Authors Conference.com, in addition to posting every newly released title on Infinity's popular online bookstore at www.BuyBooks OnTheWeb.com (www.BBOTW.com). Infinity is the founder, producer, and sole sponsor of www.AuthorNation.com —a very active social-networking website with a free and open membership for all authors, writers, poets, and book lovers—and it's totally free of third-party commercial advertising. But, of course, members are welcome to promote their books, participate in forums, post portfolios of their work, share critiques, brag a bit about promotional achievements, and exchange ideas—just like you'd do in any community of friendly people sharing similar interests and desires.

Broad distribution for every version of your book

At Infinity, we start you off on the road to sales success by providing you with the broadest distribution possible for a variety of possible versions of your book, including print book, eBook and audio. Our state-of-the-art print-on-demand technology makes it possible to fulfill book orders in a timely manner, meaning your readers never have to wait long to receive and read your book.

Our ever-expanding channels of book distribution span the globe and include two of the largest distributors in the world, Ingram Book Company and Baker & Taylor. These two companies can make your book available to over 50,000 booksellers—both online and brick-and-mortar stores. In addition, unlike most other nontraditional publishers (ask them about this), we have a direct relationship with Amazon and ship directly to their distribution network.

Infinity is dedicated to the sale of your book—which means publishing your book in whatever versions best surpass the expectations of your readers and/or listeners. Increasingly, book sales are shifting to electronic books, or eBooks, and we can now format your book perfectly for an ever-expanding array of popular eBook readers. We are the only publisher that guarantees the high quality of our electronic conversions—just as we guarantee the superior quality of every book we produce. The potential market for your book expands significantly when it's available for purchase 24/7 as an eBook download from the vast horizon of the Internet. Our global eBook distribution network encompasses over thirty-one major online retailers, including Amazon, Barnes & Noble, Books-a-Million, Chapters-Indigo, Sony, and many other points of distribution. Our eBooks are compatible with all major readers, such as the Kindle, iPad, Nook, Sony and many others.

Professional custom-designed color covers

Cover design plays an increasingly important role in sales and have been shown to increase with a compelling front and back cover and professional interior design. Infinity's unmatched custom cover and design capabilities provide real impact and are unequaled in quality, affordability, and optimization expertise. Many of our competitors will allow you to construct your cover using a template, only offer front-cover design, or limit the designer's time and/or type and number of images you can include. Using templates requires a lot of guesswork on your part and there's no way to tell what the result will be. You may end up with an inferior cookie-cutter design and have to pay a premium for a much more expensive "package" that allows your input.

Print-on-Demand—an educated choice

When you publish your book with Infinity you make an educated choice—to be part of the changing dynamics sweeping across the publishing industry. In fact, in 2009, there were more on-demand published titles than those from traditional publishers. *If you publish with Infinity, your book is not self-published.* You've granted Infinity permission to publish and distribute your book in exchange for royalties on each book sold. There is only one publisher of record of your book and that's Infinity; however, at times we will co-publish with another publisher or include a previously truly self-published author's publishing company's house name.

Infinity's one-time setup fee is for Infinity's professional services rendered to add your submitted book file into our book-publishing system and seed your book's basic information into established distribution channels. The ISBN identifies Infinity as the publisher of record. The only "self" involved is the "self-promotion" that's necessary to generate a buzzing interest in your Infinity-published book.

In reality, much like a traditional publisher, Infinity covers the cost of producing at no cost to you for the on-shelf inventory we maintain for all Infinity titles—this assures that all ordered books (whether we have inventory on hand or are produced to order) are usually shipped within 7 to 10 days from receipt of the order. Nor do we charge our authors for the cost of producing and shipping books directly to Amazon. Just like other mainstream publishers, we accept returns from bookstores—at no cost to Infinity authors—because we underwrite this program that makes our titles more acceptable for bookstores. It also facilitates authors doing in-store book signings, knowing their books are in stock to sell in conjunction with the events. Infinity's profit comes from selling books—not from selling "publishing services" of questionable value.

Maximizing your promotional effort

We recognize the importance of our authors' promotional efforts to spread the word about their books. It's these efforts that convert reader interest into increased word-of-mouth and account for accumulating sales. At Infinity, we support these efforts in numerous ways, beginning with our high-speed digital printing, online distribution, and low-cost eBook readers. Through these advances, we better support our authors' promotional efforts and open up more book distribution opportunities for all.

Even though we have published over six thousand Infinity titles, we gladly review and make cost-effective suggestions to marketing plans put together by our authors. We listen when authors want to share their marketing ideas with us. In fact, we offer a free blog for any of our authors to share their marketing successes and information about their books.

Some of our serious and motivated authors attend Infinity's annual Authors' Conference or single-day seminars. During our "Gathering of Authors" conference the last weekend in September, we have nationally acclaimed publishing professionals as our keynoters and expert presenters. The entire focus for the weekend is on teaching authors more savvy ways to provide effective promotional exposure for their books. New to our educational schedule, we are proud to have been selected by Pearl S. Buck International to deliver seminars at their writing conferences on the changing industry and our author-originated publishing method.

Extending the life cycle of your book

Another way we support your effort is by producing your book in the shortest possible time and extending its life cycle. In traditional publishing the pre-publication phase can take 12 to 18 months or longer—and then the book has a brief window of a few months to produce projected retail sales. If a book is not generating its anticipated sale, it soon goes out of print. At Infinity, it's the reverse: our pre-publication phase is usually completed in just 6 to 8 weeks. Once the book is approved for sale by the author, the book is instantly made available for sale to the public, and because the book will never go out of print, it's producing sales year after year and earning continuous royalties for promotion-minded and motivated authors.

At Infinity, our operating premise has always been, and always will be, that each one of our titles has the potential to become a steady revenue producer for its author and for Infinity. Never in the history of Infinity have we removed a book from our publishing system because of low sales. We firmly believe in every author's right to have his or her book available for purchase by the public. That's the essence of our author-friendly publishing model that clearly sets Infinity apart from all the other publishers.

Part 2

YOU'RE THE AUTHOR. YOU OWN THE CONTENT. CONTENT IS OMNIPOTENT.

Content is omnipotent, and Infinity authors create and control the content. At Infinity, writers enjoy a more expressive style, knowing their creations will be published verbatim as written. There's a freeing artistic difference when you're not writing to appease an agent into tempting interest from a mainstream house with a possible opening in their schedule at the end of next year.

Three Types of Content to Consider

When you're selling or buying real estate, the three most important factors are location, location, and location. The location of real estate is solidly fixed in place and not likely to be relocated without a natural earth-changing act of God.

When you're writing, selling, or buying a book, the three most vital elements are compelling content, focused content, and refined content. Content is fluid, always changing through the writing skills of the author creating a book, forever depicting more shared concepts with each turn of the page, endlessly beckoning the reader to learn more from the writer's words captured between the covers.

Compelling Content

Hook a reader's interest to buy your book. An attractive cover might first attract the eye, but it's the promise of what is between the covers that will sway the reader to buy. More recently, cover text has become even more important as search engines and online bookstores look at titles and other content to help buyers search for their area of interest using keywords.

Focused Content

Fulfill the promise of delivering to your readers what they want to learn about the topic of your nonfiction book, or the entertaining make-believe reality of the plot in your novel. Whenever focus strays, there's a clear and present danger of losing your reader.

Refined Content

Be sure to focus on the fine art of making your book as error free of typos, grammatical issues, and tangled thoughts as it can be. Readers expect to enjoy a smooth-reading book that has been completely purged of annoying word bumps and obnoxious mistakes.

Indeed, it is the perceived value of the content to your reader—more than anything else—that determines the success of your book. This section explains the ins and outs of content from Infinity's viewpoint and why certain types of content should be avoided.

Content Areas to Watch

There are certain uses of content that will not be accepted and will usually impede the timely release of your book or cause it to be withdrawn from publication. We do reserve the right to remove books from Infinity's book-publishing system and distribution channels if a post-publication problem develops.

Plagiarism

Copying from others is a major no-no that could result in legal action for copyright infringement brought by the original author of the work in question. Borrowing material or building on the published work of other authors will get you in trouble—unless, prior to publication, you have secured written permission from the author of the previously published work, and in some cases permission from their publisher, to use specifically defined portions and references about their work with clearly acknowledged credits. Likewise, the unauthorized quoting of even a few lines of someone's published work or work-in-progress without their written permission is unwise. A mention in the acknowledgement with the belief the originating author will appreciate the exposure of being referred to in your book is also not acceptable.

Litigious Writing and Content

Naturally, it is essential that you avoid anything that might constitute libelous statements that could result in legal actions against you—keep in mind that damages are awarded on the perceived harm done to the affronted person's reputation and loss of income. Being found guilty of libel could be costly.

Copyrighted Song Lyrics

Using copyrighted song lyrics in a book most often involves written permission and can be costly. In some cases, you may be required to pay in advance a percentage of projected book sales to the songwriter, composer, and performer. The expense for using a few lines from a popular song could quickly total several hundred dollars paid out before the first book is sold. Unless song lyrics play a vital part in your book, they are best to be avoided or be prepared to pay dearly for them. Song titles and book titles may be used only as titles without permission under the fair use prevision of US copyright law.

Fact-Checking of Content and Source Material

Some books require fact-checking to verify that facts stated in the book are truthful and correctly presented. Securing permission to use the portions of the work by others and fact-checking your book is solely your responsibility. This can be a prolonged and tedious process that Infinity does not include in its offering. We do, however, require that you provide us with appropriate documentation regarding granted permissions prior to the release of the book.

Famous People, Places, and Real Things

Most novelists include references to real people, living or dead, to add touches of reality to their plotted storyline. Public figures, elected officials, and famous people are usually okay to make mention of, as long as it's done in a positive way that isn't demeaning. Always employ common sense when using the names of real people in novels; don't assume they will be flattered by being included in your book. If you've based created characters on people you know, it's wise to obscure their identity by changing how they are portrayed in your novel. When in doubt, err on the side of caution, by leaving identifying features and unique traits out that could be linked back to the person you know.

Places are pretty much fair game. It's okay to write, "The family fleeing from the bad guys stopped at McDonald's for lunch," or "The United flight was late landing at PHL due to a weather delay." Thankfully, the days have passed when the name of the airline had to be something made up like Transnational Airways, and McDonald's was reduced to being referred to as a popular fast-food restaurant. Of course, if you're writing about the plane being infested with rats, it's best to invent the name of an imaginary airline. Likewise, if you're writing about the ghost that haunts the drive-up window—it's best to conjure up a different name for the restaurant.

Real things often have brand names attached to them. Here, common usage usually prevails, so it's okay to write, "His drink of choice was Pepsi," rather than referring to it as "soda pop," which was always seen as rather lame. However, avoid using brand names in the title of your book unless written permission has been secured. Some corporations get rather testy about having their cherished and profitable brand names incorporated into the title of books. Referencing brand names in your text only in passing is usually okay, but definitely not as an op-ed opportunity to bash and slam the product or corporate brand.

Artwork and Photographs

Do not use any artwork or photographs without comprehensive permission from the artist or photographer, and in some cases permission of identifiable people shown in the photo. People can get very sensitive about having their likeness published in a book—especially when they discover this transgression after the book has been published and is being distributed. Downloading photos and graphics from someone's website for use in your book or on your book-dedicated website is unacceptable—even if there is no apparent notice of copyright, the work could still benefit from copyright protection.

If you've had your author's head-and-shoulder photo taken by a professional portrait photographer, you will need the photographer's written permission to use any copyrighted photo of you in the promotion of your book—most likely, you'll need to pay a usage fee in addition to what you have already paid for the photo shoot. Unless of course, you have a free-use certificate from the photographer, then you can do as you please with your photo.

Your Book Published Word-for-Word Just as You Wrote it

With due consideration given to the potential content problem areas explained above, Infinity's goal is to publish your book precisely the way you wrote it and submitted it to us for publication. You, the author, have total control over your book from cover-to-cover—as long as the book formatting conforms to our production requirements. (See part 3 for instructions.)

When you publish your book with Infinity, you are granting us permission to publish and distribute your book—you retain all rights. Therefore, we can't change a single word in your book without your expressed written approval. The only exception to this policy is if you utilize Infinity's optional copyediting services. Even then, the author still has the final say on any questionable changes before approving their proof book for publication. Of equal importance, because there's no question as to the ownership of the book, only the author can determine if and when to sell off movie rights, mass market rights, foreign rights, etc.

Our First Amendment Guarantee

Infinity is a First Amendment Press; this means we will publish almost any book on any topic, in any genre, by any author. As a responsible publisher, however, we reserve the right to reject content such as, but not limited to, hate material, pornography, exploitation of children, writings advocating or depicting illegal activities, slanderous claims, and zealous rants.

We will decline the publication of work that in our opinion could result in legal action against the author and publisher. Unfortunately, we live in a time where people file seemingly frivolous lawsuits if they believe they can profit from such actions.

Upon receipt of your book file and Publishing Agreement, if Infinity's decision is not to publish, a full refund will be promptly made and your book file returned.

Freedom of Expression

We solidly support freedom of expression tempered with common sense. As an author, you have complete freedom to tell your story your way, to approach nonfiction topics with your unique angle, to be as creative as you please with your prose. Some publishers impose "house" style and usage sheets for their authors to adhere to; such requirements are not imposed on authors publishing with Infinity. However, we strongly recommend that all writers follow the accepted guidelines in style and usage manuals, in addition to working with a professional editor, to make their book the very best writing it can be—well-edited books generally sell better.

Professional Copyediting of Your Words

Professional copyediting is the essential finishing process before publication that will purge your content of typos, grammatical errors, and fix punctuation problems. This isn't the time to impose on the English teacher you met at a PTA meeting a few years ago, or ask a writer friend you know from chatting with online, to take on the copyediting task—you need a professional copy editor with experience in editing work for publication.

Don't believe you can edit your own work or trust your spellchecker to connect typos—actually that should be *correct* typos—but a spellchecker program wouldn't catch it because it's only checking the spelling and not how the word is being used. Perhaps the most embarrassing thing an author can hear from a reader is "Do you know you have a typo in the second paragraph on page 36?"

The copyediting of your book is performed before the manuscript goes into production and you will have the opportunity to approve all changes. Of course, you will also be responsible for all changes you make or sign off on as they appear in the proof copy of your book. If the editor has any questions about what you are trying to express, you will be able to review queries and make any corrections you wish to make in the manuscript. This is a valuable process as it allows you to learn from a professional and improve your writing skills. While we can't require you to have your book professionally copyedited, we hope you will take advantage of this opportunity to make your book the best it can be.

Finish Writing Your Book

Without a doubt, the most challenging—and, yes, even extremely frustrating—determination an author needs to make is to know when the process of writing (plus rewriting and rewriting some more) has reached the end point.

Perhaps you've shared your final draft with family, friends, and peers for comments—when a book is a work-in-progress nearing completion, it seems everyone wants to play editor and make changes. Yes, you've carefully considered their input, and maybe even incorporated some of their worthy suggestions, but this is not the time to embark on one more tedious rewrite. As helpful as these folks might be, they're only giving you their opinion on what they'd do differently with the content of *your book*. If you, the author, are reasonably comfortable and satisfied with the sequence, pacing, and flow of your content, and corrected the typos your reader friends have pointed out, then, by all means, proclaim your book ready to be published.

Part 3

MANUSCRIPT TO SUBMITTED BOOK FILE

You've heard the term *what you see is what you get* and that's very true of on-demand printing. The formatted book file you create for submission to Infinity is basically the way your book will appear in print—word-for-word just as you wrote it. However, before we can work our conversion magic that produces the special digitized file we print from, you must first assemble all the parts of your book into one single document that begins with your title page and ends with the last page of your book.

You Have Three Submission Options at This Point in The process

1. Use our Authors Concierge™ service and one of our Author Advocates will walk you through the entire publishing process. (You receive a 10 percent discount using this service.)

2. Send us your finished book file (without formatting) together with a sample internal and chapter page design or photographs of a design you like.

3. Format the document yourself as described below and submit your assembled book file.

Preparing for Self-Formatting

For those who wish to do it themselves, this next section provides a broad step-by-step guideline for formatting and assembling the book file. As stated above, our experienced designers will provide this formatting for you; however, we find that it sometimes benefits authors to at least do a portion of the work, if only to get an idea of how their manuscript will look in the trim size they've selected for their book. This can be an exciting process, after writing and editing your book on screen for weeks and months on end. Finally, seeing it in "book layout" can be a reward that's worth the effort.

Regardless of what word-processing program you used to write your book, the basics are relatively the same for successfully completing the "some assembly required" part of the make-ready for publication process. Infinity's production department maintains an extensive array of word-processing programs—ranging from first versions through the most recent, updated versions. There are several rather pricey commercial software programs on the market, especially for creating the layout and design of the text pages of books; however, most of these programs are complex, have a high learning curve, and require an understanding of the basic elements of effective page design. Of course, you could hire a professional graphic artist to do the layout and design of your book, and employing their services will provide you with a completed book file properly formatted for submission. But why do that when Infinity will do it for you?

If you are unsure about how to complete any of the following instructions, click on your word processor's "Help" tab for directions on how to accomplish these basic procedures. Below, we offer fundamental instructions for the Microsoft Word 2007 program.

For an example in Word 2007, perform a "save" on all of your files before beginning the formatting phase. Open a new blank document and click on "Page Layout" on the top of your open document menu. It will display "Margins" and click on the arrow to offer options to revise your margins to Infinity's specifications (bottom for "Custom Margins").

Establish a page size for your book in the Margins section, under "Custom Margins/Paper": 5.5" x 8.5"—the industry standard for trade books; 8" x 8"—for more creative forms of expression, such as poetry, photo studies, children's books, and collections of work; 8.5" x 11"—preferred for school textbooks, instructional manuals, and business topics. Under the "Paper" tab in the Custom Margins, set page size for a 5.5" x 8.5" book (for instance), with margins at least 0.7" left/right and 0.6" top/bottom; and at least at 0.8" for all margins on 8" x 8" and 8.5" x 11". For additional white space the margins can be increased slightly, but not *less* than the margin measurements shown here. White space brings breathing space for paragraphs—pages with small text and paragraph indents, instead of a smaller bit of paragraph spacing, appear crammed together to lower the printed page count, but fail at being an inviting page to read.

The second step is to simply copy-and-paste individual parts and/or chapters of the manuscript into one large book file you are about to create. Save your final manuscript file before you "select all" or highlight the entire text of the file and click "copy." Open your newly created blank book file, position the cursor in the upper left-hand corner at the top of the page and select "special paste" and from the drop-down menu select "Formatted (RTF-Rich Text Format)"—this will insert the text into your new book file document without copying editing notes, embedded codes, etc.

Continue copying and pasting one chapter after another, until all parts of your book file have been pasted in place on your newly created document. Click on "Select All" and select the type font and point size—keep baby boomers in mind with specific attention paid to the ease of readability and select a point size that's 11 or 12 points with appropriate paragraph spacing. The text of most books are hyphenated and justified, so now is the time to select these options and apply them to your book file. Save and close your manuscript file and save your newly-pasted-together book file.

The third step is a bit more involved. If you don't have a title page, dedication, Foreword/Preface/Introduction, Table of Contents, Acknowledgments, etc., comprising the typical front matter, insert the appropriate pages in front of your first chapter and add the necessary text for these pages at this time with a page break at the bottom (at the end of all text) of each page. If your first chapter doesn't begin on a right-hand page, you might want to add a blank page to make that alignment happen. At the conclusion of the first chapter, add a page break, and continue on to the end of each chapter, adding page breaks.

For the fourth step, open the "Header" and insert page numbers—the program will automatically number your pages in sequence; there is an option to retain the sequence but not number the first page of chapters. Don't worry if the page numbers don't align perfectly with the Table of Contents—Infinity's production team can fix them and everything will be correct when you receive your proof books (make a note to ask for assistance with page numbers in your submission cover letter). While the "Header" editing window is open, you can add a running header in the top margin area, such as the author's name on the left-hand page and the book title on the right-hand page—skipping adding a "header" on the first page of each chapter.

The finalizing fifth step is fine-tuning your book file. Now is the time for you to add photographs, graphics, illustrations, or design elements such as the fancy ones used to enhance chapter pages, end-of-chapter pages, or tastefully sprinkled as needed throughout the book.

There's no charge if you scan, crop, scale to size, and position your artwork appropriately on the proper pages just where you want it to be. This can be accomplished by clicking on the "insert" tab of your word processor—if the positioning doesn't align as you want it to, just click "undo" and try again. If you become totally frustrated or just don't want to do this work, we can do the positioning of photos and artwork for you; however, if our production department handles this task according to your written instructions there is a $10 charge per item. It is best to provide digitized copies of the artwork if possible; however, if you provide us with "hard copies," all photos and artwork will be promptly returned after you have approved the final proof copies of your book. Even if your images or artwork are embedded in your book file, it's always wise to include copies of your digitized photos and artwork on the CD or flash drive with your submitted book file.

If you are embedding images or artwork in your book file, make sure that they are formatted as a 200 dpi JPG. To make sure that the image does not have to be resized, you should make sure that your image is not larger than 4.1" x 7.9" for a 5.5" x 8.5" book size, 6.4" x 6.4" for an 8" x 8" book size, and 6.4" x 9.4" for an 8.5" x 11" book size.

If you are going to have your book indexed, add the keywords to use for indexing to a blank page at the end of your book file, but do not attempt to have the indexing by page numbers accomplished until you have the final proof copy of your book because the pages could change during the copyediting and conversion process. It might be better to hire a professional indexer to handle this important last phase of your book. We do not provide indexing services; however, we can dovetail the indexing of your book into the final production process of your book at no additional cost.

At this point in the process, if you do a page preview of your newly assembled book file, what you see will be very representational of how your book will appear in print. You are, of course, free to hire your own professional graphic artist to enhance the layout, design, and appearance of your book. Most graphic artists will provide you with an estimate based on your book file, and a link to their website with samples of recent work. They will develop a unique design that works well with the genre and/or topic of your book—if your book is being indexed, the book designer will also dovetail this procedure into the design process, so the end product will be correctly indexed with appropriate page numbers. The completed book file from the graphic artist will be ready for submission to Infinity. Of course, if you are the creative type and familiar with book layout, your own design is welcome.

Recently, Infinity has added a full-color interior option. If you plan to publish your book in full or partial color, you have the option of embedding full-color photographs and graphics in your book file. Keep in mind that digitally printed color is what is typically referred to as "pleasing colors"—meaning it is not going to be a perfect match to the specific shade of red or hue of blue you might envision—but the digitally printed colors will be pleasingly close. This also applies to printing of our custom-color covers, included in Infinity's one-time setup fee. Our custom-color covers are always pleasing to the eye, although there may be some slight variation in the cover colors printed at different times.

Submitting Your Book File to Infinity

You have several options when you save your book to a CD or to a USB flash drive. If you are absolutely certain everything in your book file is precisely the way you want it, you can submit it as a PDF and we will not change a thing. With your book file saved as a PDF, however, we cannot perform any copyediting, correct formatting problems, or convert your printed book file into eBook versions. Therefore, if you are submitting your book file as a PDF and you want an eBook version, you will need to include a copy of the word-processor document that was the original source file used to create the PDF book file. The most common submission format is as a word-processing document file. Almost any word-processor-document-saved book file will be compatible with Infinity's digital conversion process for printed books and eBooks.

In addition to the book file saved as a word.doc file and/or a PDF, you will also need to provide the following files on your CD or USB flash drive:

- ❏ a 30-word high-impact blurb about your book

- ❏ a 100-word synopsis describing the essence of your book

- ❏ a 100-word author biography providing facts about the author that are relevant to the book

- ❏ Also very important is the 1,000-word excerpt that is usually the first chapter of a novel or the Table of Contents with a selected chapter representational of the nonfiction book.

Just as we can't change a word in your book, we cannot edit these descriptive items for creating interest in your book on the Internet. If you exceed the word counts, your text will abruptly end at the specified word limits. It is essential that you do not exceed the specified word counts.

You can include a .jpg (image) of an optional head-and-shoulder photograph of the author, with permission to use documentation from the photographer, and photo credit line if appropriate. The author's photo on the back cover is recommended because readers like to see what the author looks like.

After everything has been saved to the CD or flash drive for submission, take the time to verify that each file opens and the entire book file is actually present, along with the supporting files about your book. Nothing is more frustrating for an author on the verge of having a book published than to receive a call from Infinity with the news that files won't open. The last thing to do is to make a backup copy of the CD or flash drive you are submitting. Now you have a duplicate CD containing all of the essential components of your book to keep in a safe place, just in case something happens to your CD or flash drive while in transit.

Congratulations! You have successfully assembled your book file and it is ready to submit to Infinity. We are frequently asked if it is acceptable to submit work via e-mail. Although we do accept e-mail submissions, we encourage authors to download their work to a CD or flash drive and submit via regular mail, if at all possible. This is because e-mail submissions are more susceptible to issues of transmission or loss than files safely stored on a CD or flash drive. Should you wish to submit via e-mail, consult your Author Advocate or in-house support person for specific submission instructions. Regardless of how you choose to submit, we recommend saving all documents.

We're in Agreement

For the publishing process to officially begin, you will also need to submit along with your book file a signed copy of Infinity's Publishing Agreement—the document you received along with this publishing guide. The document may also be downloaded from our website, as can other agreements pertaining to ancillary rights or copyediting. This straightforward document explains the terms and conditions of our jointly-entered-into agreement, and defines the responsibilities of the author and publisher to mutually profit from the publication of your book.

As you review Infinity's Publishing Agreement, you'll see it's very transparent, straightforward, and easy to understand. However, we will be glad to answer any questions with specific regard to your book and Infinity's terms and conditions for publishing. Our goal is to provide you with a comfortable, author-friendly, profitable publishing experience.

When you are comfortable with the terms of the agreement, we ask that you send us a signed copy along with your completed order form. In most cases, these documents should be returned to Infinity along with the required book file and support materials, although for some special promotions, we allow authors to sign up and then submit their book file at a later date. If you have trouble completing your agreement or just wish for additional support, your Author Advocate can help you complete the agreement by phone and even take your credit card information and process your order. You will still have to print out and sign a hard copy of your publishing agreement or send Infinity a copy that has been signed electronically.

What to Expect and How to Proceed

One and a half to three months typically elapses between the time we receive your submission and the time your book is available for sale on our website. This includes:

❑ about three to four weeks for you to receive your first eProof book. During this time period you will receive emails form us as your Book moves through the pre-publishing process

- a couple of weeks for you to thoroughly proofread your book

- about two weeks for us to ship a corrected proof book

- more proofreading time on your end before you send your signed proof approval form back to us

- final wrap-up as the book is prepared to print

In most cases, there are several types of corrections to be made to the first proof. A second proof book is almost always necessary to get your book up to your standards of what it should be.

Please understand that files that have inconsistent formatting, that aren't edited before being submitted to us, or that use unusual fonts not included on the disk can increase the time it takes to publish a book.

Authors frequently see grammar and spelling problems pop right off the pages of their first proof books, perhaps due to seeing the work in book form for the first time. Delays and extra fees can be avoided by sending a thoroughly edited and proofread book.

Published books will be available for sale on our website within two weeks after the book is approved and all corrections have been made. When your book is cleared for printing, you will receive notice by e-mail.

If you have any questions relevant to the submission of your book or any material contained in this book, don't hesitate to call us at our toll free number 1.877.BUY.BOOK (289-2665)

Part 4

THE PUBLISHING PROCESS BEGINS

Nothing can start the process of publishing your book until your submission arrives at Infinity. Unlike many other publishers, we welcome new submissions daily—we always have openings in our publishing schedule for what could become Infinity's next up-and-coming steady seller. Upon arrival of your book file, several sequential processes are completed concurrently to produce eProof copies of your book in a timely fashion—typically within 3 to 4 weeks. The following is an approximation of the steps involved when Infinity publishes your book. However, do not fret, we will be sending you email notifications throughout each step of the publishing process.

Verifying Submitted Files

When your book file and publishing agreement are received, we check your book file to verify it opens and the file contains the entire book and requested promotional info files. We'll promptly acknowledge the acceptance of your submission and let you know if there's a problem with the file not opening.

ISBN Assigned

We assign you an in-house Author Representative when we officially log your book into the production schedule, and assign an International Standard Book Number (ISBN)—several digits identify Infinity as the publisher of record. This unique control number is like a Social Security number identifying your book and all book transactions from release to current. If you have selected our optional Library of Congress Control Number (LCCN) and US Copyright Registration service, for Infinity to handle these government filings, the process of preparing and submitting the paperwork to secure an LCCN is started at this time.

Copyediting

If you have wisely decided to utilize Infinity's copyediting service or one of the services associated with Book Genesis, then at this time your book file is professionally edited and sent to you for final review and approval. We make the process author-friendly by providing you with two copies of your manuscript—one a PDF copy showing the "tracked changes" and the other a Word document with all changes made. You have the opportunity to accept or reject changes made by the copyeditor.

Make-Ready Formatting

When your book moves to our pre-production department adjustments are made as needed to correct any formatting problems, adjust table of content numbers to align with actual page number, and tweak the formatting to make it the very best it can be. During this phase, any photographs and graphics to be included in your book are scanned, cropped, sized, and positioned on the pages you indicate. You will be contacted if there is any uncertainty about what to position where. We welcome your written instructions explaining any specific parts of your book needing our gentle attentive touch to make everything right.

Professionally Created Cover Art

Infinity's graphics department creates custom cover art especially for your book. We are guided by your suggestions and synopsis, and our masterful graphic designers will be in touch with you directly if they have any questions regarding the development of the artwork that will grace the cover of your book. If you have prepared your own cover artwork, we are able to use it but may have to modify it to meet the production requirements for printing full-color covers. However, we reserve the right to reject submitted artwork that we consider doesn't do justice to the book or appears amateurish.

Book File Conversion, Printing, and Binding

Now your book file is converted into the unique file that Infinity's high-speed digital printers need to print your book (the process of printing books in color can take longer as converting and creating color digital print files is more complex and requires additional attention to achieve pleasing color). These marvelous monsters can digitally print a complete 300-page black-and-white book in less than a minute. The interior pages and full-color, laminated softcovers are married together with perfect binding. If you are utilizing Infinity's CD-inside-the-book feature, the envelope containing the CD is added to the back cover and trimmed to the selected size. The interior pages destined for hard covers—with optional dust jackets—have a more involved bindery process. Additionally, if you are publishing an eBook or audio book, we will convert your document to the standard format required for ingestion into our global eBook and audio distribution network. If you're ever in the West Conshohocken area near Philadelphia, Pennsylvania, call for an appointment to stop by our facilities and we'll gladly show you how we produce books.

eProof Books Sent

Your first proof will be in the format of an eProof in PDF format. However, the *formatting* of your eProof book may be a little different from how it had looked on your computer. This is very common when a file is transferred from one computer to another. The text will not change, but the format of it may (this is not the case for PDF or hardcopy-only submission). Therefore your eProof book will ultimately be a representation of what your book looks like when we have it open on our computer and have fixed any obvious problems. We will make the necessary correction to your book. Any problems that cannot be fixed with the 1st eProof book will be fixed for the 2nd eProof book, etc. At the end of this process, the author has the ability to order a Printed proof copy of their Book.

Advance Reading Copies Shipped

If you've had the foresight to order the Advance Reading Copy (ARCs) program, then 24 glitch-free proof books with "Advance Reading Copy" printed across the front and back covers will be sent to you with your production proof books.

Carefully Proofing Your Proof Books

The sole purpose of the proof book is for you to verify word-for-word everything about your book is correct and just as you wrote it. Follow the proof reviewing instructions, sent with the Proof Approval form, about how to indicate and make note of typos and minor alterations. These will be changed and made right by Infinity prior to your book being released for sale. We will make up to 40 changes at no charge on the initial proof books; however, after 40 changes and with additional proofing, there is an additional cost. If at any time more than 20 corrections are made, a revised set of proof books will be promptly sent to you. This is not the time to embark on an extensive rewrite—or for that matter, even a minor rewrite. You, the author, have the responsibility to carefully read your proof book before signing and returning the Proof Approval form to Infinity. The Proof Approval form must be in our physical possession before your book will be made available for sale and posted to various bookseller websites.

ISBN Registration

Upon your authorization to release your book for sale, Infinity registers the book's ISBN with R.R. Bowker's Books In Print—this is the identifying number we assigned to your book at the beginning of the publishing process. The Bowker listing includes the English-speaking country of origin, identifies Infinity as the publisher of record, and basic information about the book with publisher contact info for book buyers. Infinity's publisher's listing notes every title sold by Infinity to booksellers is guaranteed returnable at no cost to our authors.

Internet Website Pages

We produce three web pages presenting information about your book on Infinity's online bookstore, BuyBooksOnTheWeb.com. There is a page featuring your book cover—the cover enlarges when you put the cursor on the front cover of your book. There's also a section that includes basic information about page count, format size, copyright date, and a 100-word synopsis to generate reader interest from the abstract about your book. For potential buyers wanting a taste of your writing style, there's a 1,000-word sneak peek you provided with your submission. The biography provides a brief insight into your background as the author—this is something most readers want to know. Authors are encouraged to create and maintain their own book-dedicated website to provide more complete information about the book and the author's background.

Amazon's Advantage Program

Every Infinity title is automatically enrolled in Amazon's Advantage program at no cost to the author. Infinity provides Amazon with the initial on-shelf inventory that assures your book's listing is shown in stock and available for immediate delivery from Amazon. The mighty Amazon is the largest bookstore in the entire universe—their prime advantage is of the sheer number of shoppers and transactions occurring through their website every day. Amazon customers are attracted by the promise of their content, carrying over 90 percent of all books in print and/or available in digital versions currently published and posted for sale worldwide. Amazon will usually post your newly released book to their website within 10 to 14 business days after your book is posted on the BuyBooksOnTheWeb.com website. Amazon uses their Internet analytics to determine how much to discount your book. Under the terms of the Advantage program, Amazon buys Infinity titles at a discount off the retail price. This margin allows Amazon to discount books as they desire. Indeed, you are now a published author: your content has been produced as a book and made available for purchase by everyone in the world with access to the Internet and Amazon.com.

On-Shelf Micro-Inventory Maintained

We produce the initial inventory of your book which enables us to promptly ship most book orders within 24 to 48 hours, and whenever possible the same day the orders are received. These inventoried books are produced at no cost to you—this is an investment we make in you and your book. We do not charge a maintenance fee to keep your book in our publishing and distribution system or to maintain your on-shelf inventory. Like you, we have a continuing investment and an ongoing interest in the success of your book.

eBook Conversion and Distribution

If you selected Infinity's eBook conversion program, your book file is now being converted and produced in eBook versions (ePUB or PRC)—formatted for sale and distribution by Infinity through the major outlets, including Amazon's Kindle, Sony e-readers, Border's e-reader, B&N's nook, iPad/iPod, BLIO, and all reader-empowered smartphones. If you submitted your book file as a PDF, you'll need to provide the word.doc file that was the source of the PDF to convert to an eBook. Once the eBook conversion has occurred, it's virtually future-proof, meaning we have the ability to adapt eBook versions to be compatible with any new readers that become available in the future.

Ingram/Lightning Source Global Print Distribution

If you've selected Infinity's Extended Distribution option, at this time in the process, with your authorization and payment of the $199 fee, we provide Lightning Source with the digital file reformatted to their specifications that will be added to their databases of available titles—providing over 50,000 book sellers access to purchase your book. Lightning Source produced books are noted in their databases as nonreturnable; likewise, only Infinity books produced in-house are covered by Infinity's guaranteed return policy for bookstores.

US Copyright Filing

If Infinity is handling your filing for US Copyright certification and protection with the Library of Congress, with your authorization and payment of $150 which includes the Library of Congress Control Number (LCCN) registration service, the final approved edition of your book is submitted with the supporting paperwork at this time. Although Infinity is taking care of the paperwork, the author is always identified as the owner of the content and sole holder of the copyright. It could take three to six months or longer to receive the official LOC certification; however, your creative efforts are protected under the revised US Copyright law as soon as you started writing your book.

Complimentary Books

Infinity includes at least five complimentary copies of your newly published book with your first book order—which is at 50 percent off the suggested retail price to adjust fairly for author-authorized value-added pricing. Future orders by the author are at 40 percent off the suggested retail price—royalties of 10 percent are paid on all purchases by the author. We have no minimum; however, orders for 250 or more books are always at 50 percent off the suggested retail price. Infinity pays UPS ground shipping charges on all orders for 25 or more books and only charges a $4.50 handling fee per ship-to address.

Virtual Listings with Online Booksellers

Usually within a few weeks from your book's Amazon listing, other third-party booksellers will ingest (include in their database) your book metadata (information about your book) and offer it for sale. When those booksellers with a virtual inventory receive an order for your book, they rely on Amazon or Infinity to fill the order. If these virtual booksellers are in Amazon's Affiliate program, then Amazon processes and fulfills the order as if it came from their affiliate.

Standard Distribution Channels

In addition to Amazon, your book is automatically added to the Baker & Taylor standard database and made available for sale through Barnes & Noble, and other mass-market retailers that are pulling metadata from Books In Print. We are constantly working to expand our channels of distribution for Infinity-published titles. For inclusion into all of our retail and international distribution, our Extended Distribution option provides global coverage.

Part 5

THE INFINITY POST-PUBLISHING ADVANTAGE

The nineteen procedures in the previous section are an approximation of the publishing and distribution process your book travels through when your book file arrives at Infinity. With some publishers and all book printers, this is where their process ends, except for order processing, order fulfillment, and a quarterly accounting of books sold. Infinity provides all these typical publishing, distribution, and administrative functions, but in addition, we offer unequaled post-release author support to provide the framework to help generate exposure, directly contributing to selling more books.

There's no doubt, it's your ongoing promotional effort that will help you get your book in the hands of readers. That said, we have several policies and procedures in place to support you in your effort and give you a huge leg up, providing your book with important advantages in the marketplace.

Unequalled Customer Service and Support

From a writer's initial contact with Infinity and throughout the author's entire publishing experience, we are available to answer questions by phone or e-mail regarding any aspect of the publishing process and distribution of your book. Naturally, we extend the same superior customer service when buyers order your books from Infinity. We are proud of our shipping department's outstanding performance record for shipping most book orders the same day received, or the next business day. Producing books in-house and maintaining an on-shelf inventory provides us with a timely advantage for prompt customer book-order fulfillment. The best way to evaluate what your customers will experience is to order a book directly from the publishers you are considering to publish your book.

Competitive Pricing

We establish a suggested retail price based on the actual page count of the book. The page count is the basis for calculating the production cost of digitally printing and binding the book. Thanks to our highly skilled and diligently efficient production department, our retail pricing is comparable to the cover price of softcover trade books released by more-traditional publishers. Competitive pricing enhances your book's positioning and acceptance in the marketplace. Many authors using other self-publishing services to publish their books sadly discover after the fact that their books' retail price—imposed by the publishing service—is at a much higher price than similar books, and an unattractive price to their readers.

Value-Added Pricing

This demonstrates our trust in the ability of nonfiction authors, and novelists with an established following of readers from previously published novels, to establish a fair and realistic retail price higher than the suggested price for their books. Although "content is king," it's still generally counterproductive to price a book considerably higher than similar books on the same topic—regardless of the perceived worth of the proprietary content. It's wise to stay within the range of the other books. The amount of value-added pricing determined by the author is always an increase in whole dollars (beginning at no less than $2 higher) and is subject to final approval by Infinity. The author's proportional royalty is 75 percent of the value-added increase—this is in addition to the standard earned royalty paid on the suggested retail price.

Standard Trade Discounts and Return Policy

Infinity sells books to retail bookstores at 40 percent off the cover price, guaranteed to be returnable for one year from the invoice date. This is at no cost to our authors, and royalties are paid as if the books are sold. In the event books are returned, we simply debit previously paid royalties from future-earned royalties. You will never receive a bill from Infinity to make your book fully returnable, nor will we ever invoice you for previously paid royalties received, on returned books. Books purchased through Amazon's Advantage program are sold to Amazon at a 55 percent discount, likewise infinity titles fulfilled through Ingram are also significantly discounted and NOT RETURNABLE to Infinity. Clarifying applied discounts is important for you, our author, because the percentage of royalties paid by Infinity is determined by the actual selling price of the book—which is the discounted cover price.

Retail Sales

Infinity pays you 30 percent royalties on orders placed directly with Infinity by retail customers ordering by phone, fax, or through BuyBooksOnTheWeb.com. We accept all major credit cards, and personal checks, while money orders/certified bank checks are required for overseas purchases. Most orders are shipped r within 7 to 10 business days. We have the ability to track every order shipped via UPS while in transit.

Author Discounts

Newly published authors receive a first-order 50 percent discount off the suggested retail price; thereafter, author purchases are at 40 percent off the suggested retail price. However, authors placing orders at any time for 250 or more books are always given a 50 percent discount off the suggested retail price. We pay UPS ground shipping on all orders for 20 books or more and only charge a $4.50 handling fee per ship-to address. Infinity pays a 10 percent royalty on all purchases by the author. We mean it when we say we pay monthly royalties on *all* books sold—including your books purchased by you. Many authors profitably sell a significant number of books after they've given a speech to an audience interested in their topic.

Sponsorship Discounts

We can accommodate corporations, associations, and groups making bulk purchases of your book by extending a special discount and inserting a sponsor's page. Books on topics related to their business, the mission of associations, or aligning with the special interest of groups are frequently given away by sponsoring organizations. Sponsors may order from 100 to 10,000 books and special arrangements can be made to tastefully position the sponsor's logo on the front and back cover. Our low minimum order makes this a cost-effective way for community groups to sponsor your book as a fundraising tool—this option provides positive exposure for you and is for a good cause.

Promotional Books

We reserve the right to give away, at Infinity's discretion and expense, a reasonable number of royalty-free complimentary books to promote the title and/or provide as samples of the quality of books we produce. At times we donate a bundle of appropriate books to several book festivals, reading programs, library fundraising events, and in support of SPCA activities—in addition to being author friendly, we're pet friendly, too.

Complimentary Review Copies

Infinity will a send a complimentary copy of your book with an enclosed Infinity thank-you card upon written request by book reviewers writing for verifiable publications (or other qualified media), thanking the reviewer for their interest, and that we are delighted, as the publisher, to provide a review copy on behalf of our author. If the reviewer carbon copies (CCs) you when his or her request is made, we'll CC you when we reply to the reviewer, confirming the requested book has been sent directly to the reviewer.

We do not advocate sending potential reviewers unsolicited books with hopes of the recipient writing a blurb—rarely are reviews forthcoming and these copies are likely to end up on the Internet as used books. Although, those with a known interest in your book who have previously expressed a willingness to write a review for you deserve to receive an autographed finished book sent from you, the author, with a note thanking him or her for the kind offer to share a few thoughts about your literary efforts.

Monthly Publisher's Statement

E-mailed statements are sent to you monthly, documenting all copies of your books sold during the most recent reportable month. The statement includes total number of copies sold from release to date, with a breakdown by selling prices and corresponding royalties earned. There is a time lag between the reportable month and the month when the statement is issued to allow time for accounts to be properly settled. Royalties are paid on the actual selling price: 10 percent on purchases at 40 to 50 percent off the suggested retail price by the author; 15 percent on returnable wholesale orders sold at 40 percent off cover to bookstores; 15 percent on distributor orders at 50 to 55 percent off cover; and 30 percent on all retail purchases via BBOTW.com. Royalty checks are issued when the amount of royalty due is $20 or more.

Royalty Splits

If you wrote the book with a co-author, we can split royalties and send separate checks, as well as duplicate Publisher's Statements to both individuals. Similar royalty splits can be arranged for illustrators, graphic artists, editors, agents, and book coaches, according to instructions from the primary author regarding the division of proceeds from book sales. Infinity's accounting of every book sold helps to keep both parties on the same page with accurate numbers—agreeing on a fair division of labor is up to them to work out.

Royalties Paid after the Author Has Passed On

Infinity authors may have a legal document prepared by an attorney that states upon the death of author, the deceased author's book is to continue to be published by Infinity with the royalties paid to the named individual, university, or charitable organization to whom the rights have been legally reassigned to. The legal term for this is a predetermined directed assignment—sort of like a living will for assuring the continued life of the book. In some states this will keep royalty assets from being entangled in probate proceeding and guarantee the book will never go out of print, even after the author is long gone.

Author Privacy Guaranteed

Infinity will never release any information regarding our authors or the total number of their books sold and royalties paid. However, in compliance with Internal Revenue Service requirements we will issue an IRS Form 1099 in the month of

January reporting the annual total of royalties paid to authors when the amount is $10 or more.

Customer Privacy

Under the Consumer Fair Trade Laws provision protecting customer privacy, Infinity is unable to release any information regarding our customers and their book purchases. When we receive e-mail and USPS mail sent by customers to the author, in care of Infinity, we will do our utmost to forward these communications to the author for their response.

New Bookstore Accounts

If there's an independent bookstore in your area interested in ordering your book to add to their on-shelf inventory, we will be glad to negotiate terms and open an account, and ship books to the store. Likewise, any locally owned specialty retail stores selling books are welcome to apply for an open account with Infinity. There's no need for authors to enter into consigning books and taking on the task of keeping the stores supplied, when they can order directly from Infinity, or their wholesaler. Simply ask the store manager to call Infinity to place an order.

Satisfaction Guaranteed

An astonishing 30 percent of our new titles come from authors who have published with us previously. This indicates the high degree of satisfaction we provide to authors. Once you publish with Infinity, you'll never want to publish elsewhere. We pride ourselves on your satisfaction and our adherence to a "Gold Standard" of service. Give us the opportunity to earn your trust.

Part 6

MARKET SUCCESS IS UP TO YOU

Success starts with compelling content refined by professional editors. Publishing with an author-friendly publisher provides the supportive professional platform for success. However, the sustaining surges of success flow primarily from the ongoing promotional exposure generated by the author. Indeed, exposure equals book sales!

As it was mentioned before, sales are the financial measuring rod for the success of your book.

Breakeven Point

The breakeven point is when the fee for the professional services rendered to publish, distribute, and promote your book is surpassed by earned royalties. In accountant talk, it's financially moving from expensive red ink into profit-laden black. To figure your book's breakeven point, take the total cost of bringing your book into the marketplace, for example $1,500—and divide by the average royalty earned. If you're considering a book promotion opportunity that costs $150 to participate, then you need the exposure to result in 15 books being sold before the effort produces a return on the investment, assuming that the average royalty earned is $10 per book.

Each marketing opportunity is like planting mystery seeds; you never know when the seeds will eventually sprout and draw interest in your book. For all things, there's a season—sort of—and sometimes there's no rhyme or reason to when something comes into season and yields the fruitful profit of book orders. Sometimes your promotional efforts may take longer to reach the breakeven point. As long as you keep a running total of ongoing investments in your book, you can project an overall approximation of how many books are needed to sell to recoup promotional ventures.

The point of diminishing returns occurs when a promotional thrust slows down after the purchased window of marketplace exposure expires. Sure, there will be a trickle of interest after the fact, but unless sales surpassed the breakeven point, it could be a long time in coming—but then again, some content lives forever on the Internet. When your book is always available for purchase, there's the profit potential for steadily accumulating financial returns from all your promotional efforts.

The Digital Advantage

One of the advantages of digital publishing using POD technology is the ability to swap book files and introduce a new and improved second edition whenever it's ready for release. This provides authors with the opportunity to repair damaged content and launch their revised books anew with hopes of more robust sales. Swapping book files makes updating time-sensitive information more current and greatly expands the market for books containing timely content. We do charge a nominal fee for updating book files with approximately the same number of pages as the original edition. The fee is higher if the cover price, page count, and ISBN need to be changed.

Amazon Rankings

Your book's ranking on Amazon is not always an indicator of sales, nor is it necessarily something to strive for. The numerical movements in Amazon rankings frequently reflect consumer interest in other books on the same general topic or genre as yours. When the ranking drops lower, that's usually indicative of increasing public interest in the topic, which means a few purchases of your book may be the result of the book's relativity to a timely topic of current interest.

Some authors try to improve their Amazon ranking by having family, friends, and social-networking buddies order their book from Amazon on the same day. The good news is maybe 50 or so books are sold which is enough to plunge the number; the sad news is the 15 percent earned royalty is on books consigned to Amazon at 55 percent off cover—this is how Amazon is able to discount like they do. The author's royalty would have been doubled had the cluster of orders been placed directly with BBOTW.com. The question is, do you want worthless bragging rights to an empty number, or do you want to focus on promoting your book into money? Hopefully, you'll decide on the latter.

The Meaningful Book Numbers

Some might say it's the ISBN, your book's identifying social security number that is most important to book sales. This number allows us to track your book through the sales process. The ISBN is important when sales numbers start to be linked to an increasing number of books sold—in publishing lingo, it's a book pulling or making projected sales numbers, or when it sells the number of copies necessary to earn back the cost of getting it into print. Crossing that initial breakeven point financially transforms you into an author earning a trackable income from the sale of your book.

Of course earning an income from your book is one of the reasons for publishing, in addition to expressing yourself through your writing skills. Regardless of your motivation for authoring your book, royalty revenue is indeed a worthy benefit for the author— even if it's only enough to provide for a few creature comforts. Don't go quitting your day job in anticipation of instant fame and vast fortunes from the sale of your book—it is not probable— although, there are several Infinity authors earning comfortable incomes from speaking engagements with back-of-the-room sales and promoting their books on the Internet. While a good number of authors are diligently working the market to hit breakeven and beyond, there are still a number of titles that sell less than 100 copies. The lacking sales are usually rooted in the absence of promotional efforts by the author.

Motivated authors making meaningful sales are shameless book opportunists, ever watchful for opportunities to mention their books, ready to tactfully exploit positive windows of exposure, and if need be, making their own book-hook opening, "Well, since you didn't ask, I'm an author and the title of my recent book is . . ." Naturally, it's best to smoothly interject this information into a conversation in a non-offensive way.

Books on Hand

Never leave home without a few copies of your most recent book. It's amazing how authors miss making sales simply because they didn't have a book close at hand. Oh sure, when you don't have a book with you to sell to them at the moment they're reaching for their cash, people will say they'll order your book, but very few actually follow through and place an order—although it sure does help if you have a business card or a bookmarker to remind them of their interest in your book.

Always have a supply of books on hand for those social events and holiday gatherings, so when relatives ask about your book, you'll have copies to sell them. With relatives being related to you some will expect to receive a free autographed book from you; nicely explain that selling your book is how you make a living. Then tell them you'll gladly give them, your family and friends, a special discount and knock off a few bucks to keep peace in the family.

Marketing Plans

Infinity will not develop and implement marketing plans for individual titles. However, upon request, we will review and make suggestions to improve the cost-effectiveness of marketing plans prepared by the author. We believe authors know better than we do the target market for their book and are usually the very best candidates to do the promoting that will get the word out—prospects can't consider buying your book if they don't know you have one, or what it's about.

Infinity does offer additional marketing services that include the printing of promotional material and cutting-edge services that serve those authors that are looking for something extra to launch their book or to provide a sustaining effort to their marketing program. Sometimes we will recommend marketing programs offered by trusted third parties, for Infinity authors to consider. Usually we are able to negotiate a reduced price for Infinity authors to participate because frequently these are pilot programs, and we have an excellent test bed of several thousand authors with a diverse offering of published books. At times, Infinity provides the initial seed books for authors participating in these optional programs; however, we will not provide financial support. Whenever possible, we encourage authors to talk with other authors who have engaged in similar programs, and compare notes.

Authors' Conferences and Seminars

Infinity offers superb opportunities to network with experts in the publishing community and connect with fellow authors. Traditionally held the last weekend in September in Valley Forge, Pennsylvania, this event has earned high acclaim from authors who have forged into the knowledge reservoir, for delivering more than promised. Attendees are usually surprised to discover the conference registration fee includes meals and lodging for the weekend—this way we have an in-house audience to captivate with creative concepts for selling more books. The entire focus of the conference is to teach authors the most current techniques for successfully selling their books. We do our utmost to keep the registration fee author affordable for this not-for-profit event, while generating a workable income carefully budgeted to produce a world-class conference with top-notch presenters and keynoters.

The benefit to Infinity is authors who have attended a conference sell more books—many of the authors who have been to Valley Forge return more than once to participate in this annual event that always has current topics of interest to authors. Infinity earns its profit selling books, and our authors make those sales happen—this is especially true of authors who have been part of a "Gathering of Authors" events.

Infinity is proud to be affiliated with Pearl S. Buck International in delivering Author-Originated Publishing workshops. We are always interested in hearing from our authors or partners about new opportunities to spread the word about books!

No publisher can guarantee the financial success of your book. Even books published by mainstream publishing houses and backed by thousands of advertising dollars may fail to produce the projected volume of sales. That's why it's more important than ever that authors understand their role in creating the success of their published book—regardless of how the book was published.

Part 7

TESTIMONIALS

The Infinity team takes pride in our ability to promise the kind of service our authors want and deserve. If you are a first-time author or a seasoned author, there will always be someone you can speak with that can provide the service you need. *Your satisfaction is our promise.*

From Our Authors

"The main thing I like about Infinity Publishing is that they do what they say they are going to do in the time period they say it will be done. I cannot find fault with that at all. They respond to my calls and e-mails. They send books quickly when I order them."

- Bob O'Connor, author of *The Perfect Steel Trap: Harper's Ferry 1859*

"I can say that I've always been satisfied with Infinity from the get-go when I worked with them and published my first book with them in 2003. They were reasonably priced and believed in me and coached me through the process very well. I attended their Annual Authors' Conference in 2004 as a guest speaker and got to meet their staff personally and see their office and production process. They are great, down-to-earth people. It has a family atmosphere. From what I've heard, Infinity is one of the oldest and most reputable print-on-demand publishers. I find them very friendly and responsive to my e-mails and when I order books—about 2 to 3 times per month—they get them shipped to me promptly. I have only good things to say about Infinity Publishing as a company and their staff as competent and approachable. I have referred a few friends who are authors to Infinity."

- Terrence Shulman, author of *Something for Nothing: Shoplifting Addiction and Recovery*

"Four Infinity Authors' Gatherings in four consecutive years, each time hearing exactly what we needed to hear from experts in the field to move our book forward! At our first September Infinity Gathering, our book was only a few months 'old' having been published the previous June. One of the experts in attendance had high praise for our work, giving us added hope and elevating our excitement. In the second Gathering we met our website designer and consequently developed and launched a wonderfully artistic site. Gathering number three introduced us to the world of dynamic marketing, just what we needed to hear, helping us achieve acceptance of our work by B&N. Session four, this year's Gathering, featured a high-powered dose of eBooks and why we must move in that direction. Our eBook will be available shortly. Mixing this with a broad range of fellow authors, sharing our experiences and comparing notes is an outstanding combination. As we hear each year, we are all collaborators and can work together to help each other. Infinity's Authors' Gathering is an exciting venue to meet industry experts and fellow authors and get to know them personally. The atmosphere is informal and well facilitated. Congratulations Infinity!"

- Bob Kline, author of *Wholeness in Living: Kindling the Inner Light*

"In today's complex, multifaceted, publishing industry, I found Infinity's commitment to their authors' success, combined with an individualized hands-on approach, was like finding a friend. Expert guidance, and attention to detail, made the process from manuscript submission, to distribution of books, a short adrenaline-filled process. The knowledge that I had industry-leading professionals on my team enabled me to confidently launch my novel into the market. More, I was eager to do it again and again! (And I did!) Infinity's Annual Gathering of Authors is a must-do for any writer, published or not. The wealth of knowledge packed into this unique weekend event will energize and inspire. The skills taught and tips shared provide authors with the tools they require to successfully achieve their publishing and marketing goals. This exceptional conference is yet another example of Infinity's commitment to the success of their authors."

– Laura Rudacille, author of *Here's the Thing...*

"I researched hard and long for a publisher and Infinity struck me from the beginning. Infinity Publishing presented itself as not just a business, but as 'people oriented' and people with honor and integrity. I wanted to trust that those stories would be well cared for and honored by the publisher as 'not just another book,' but as worthy of their time and care. I now know that I made a sound and great decision. When I have a concern, find an error, need something, all I need to do is let those needs be known! Infinity is there for their author (me), and I have no concerns, problems, when we are finished with the conversations. Infinity will publish my next book, there is no doubt. I am proud to be an Infinity author."

– Dr. Sherry E. Showalter, author of *Healing Heartaches, Stories of Loss and Life*

"With Infinity, publishing my book has been a great experience! Pleasant people, professional support, quality printing and a great price...I looked at many other publishers and am delighted that I chose Infinity. And there's so much more they offer; their 2010 author's conference was mentally stimulating, filled with new, very helpful ideas, great opportunities to network and meet lots of wonderful people! At the conference, information about Infinity's eBook and audio book programs really caught my interest as exciting new ways to sell my book. Looking forward to many more positive experiences with Infinity Publishing."

- Jane Hamilton, author of *Journey of a Lifetime: The Caregiver's Guide to Self-Care*

"Go with Infinity Publishing. I researched many other publishers, and Infinity made the most sense. Once I started working with them, I found that they're a great group of people, serious about my success."

- Jennifer Monahan, author of *An American in Oz: Discovering the Island Continent of AUSTRALIA*

"I had an amazing time at the 2010 'Express Yourself...' Gathering of Authors. It was a pleasure meeting the Infinity staff, presenters, and attendees. After getting back from the conference, I redesigned my website based on tips that I learned. I plan to continually add content to my site, and utilize the countless marketing techniques that I learned over the course of those three enlightening days."

- Laura Sepesi, author of *The Guardian of Kelmar*

"Infinity is the Cadillac of the industry. From the formatting to the cover, the staff has helped me so much and given me exactly what I wanted. They really are top notch."

- Robert Pelton, author of *Civil War Period Cookery*

"I've published two nonfiction books through Infinity, *How To Be a DIRT-SMART Buyer of Country Property* (2007) and *LAND MATTERS The "Country Real Estate" Columns, 2007–2009* (2010). I plan to publish a second book of columns in 2011. I like working with Infinity, because I can publish what I want rather than work my material into the cookie-cutter template of trade publishing. The time between a print-ready manuscript and publishing is a couple of weeks with Infinity versus a year or so with a trade house."

– Curtis Seltzer, author of *How to be a DIRT-SMART Buyer of Country Property*

"My experience with Infinity Publishing has truly exceeded all of my expectations. Their professionalism and attention to detail are a credit to the book publishing profession and to themselves. It is with the highest regard that I recommend Infinity Publishing to writers who may be considering self-publishing as a vehicle with which to bring their words to life."

- Edward F. Haas, author of *Beyond the Blues: Treating Depression One Day at a Time*

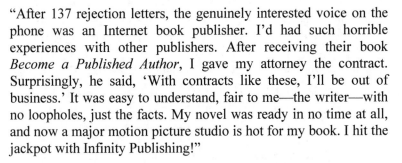

"After 137 rejection letters, the genuinely interested voice on the phone was an Internet book publisher. I'd had such horrible experiences with other publishers. After receiving their book *Become a Published Author*, I gave my attorney the contract. Surprisingly, he said, 'With contracts like these, I'll be out of business.' It was easy to understand, fair to me—the writer—with no loopholes, just the facts. My novel was ready in no time at all, and now a major motion picture studio is hot for my book. I hit the jackpot with Infinity Publishing!"

- Clarke Allan, author of *The First Man to Be First Lady*

"In sending my book to publishers, I received nice compliments. But the bottom line was 'It doesn't fit.' I almost gave up. When I received Infinity's book, *Become a Published Author*, I liked the new concept. But what I really liked was the fact that it gave me clear and definitive answers to my questions. I signed their publishing agreement and published my book. Every step has had the same courteous and efficient help. My newly published book is attractive and selling well. I am extremely satisfied with Infinity Publishing!"

- Charles J. Dobbins, author of *If Jesus Were a Sportswriter*

"I chose Infinity Publishing because I knew that my marketing efforts would not be wasted. When I'm doing talk shows, I tell the listeners, 'The quickest way to purchase my book is to call Infinity Publishing's toll-free number. They send the book out within 24–48 hours, guaranteed!' I am secure about this commitment to quick delivery because Infinity is the only large POD publisher in the U.S. that prints its own books. If people want to purchase my book but experience inconsistent fulfillment, those lost sales translate to a waste of my time and marketing efforts. Also, after purchasing some books printed by Lightning Source [Ingram's POD printing company], it was evident that the print quality of Infinity's books was much better, especially for photos. Infinity Publishing has done a great job in all aspects, and I have had nothing but good feedback from anyone I've spoken to who has purchased my book or other writers who have published with Infinity. I plan to publish all the books in my series with Infinity."

- Carol Welsh, author of *When You're Seeing Red STOP*

"I believe we're in an exciting time for the artistic world because of the Internet's distribution potential. Through the instant publishing technology used by Infinity Publishing, new ideas and literature created by and for the common man will finally be available. The information age is truly HERE!"

- Peter Quest, author of *Luminous*

"My goal was to provide our children and grandchildren with a legacy of my late husband's novel in print. Infinity Publishing provided the easiest and most economical way of doing this. The book was published within a few months of submission. Friends who ordered it received their copies within a few days. We are all very proud of the book."

- Joan M. Rinehart, author of *The Carriage Drivers*

"Travel guide information must be timely, or it is of little value. The best way to ensure the timeliness of your book is to get published with Infinity. Necessary changes can be made to update the book, and readers benefit by getting advice that is current and up to date. This would be impossible with traditional printing methods, where thousands of previously printed books would instantly become useless."

- Anne Korff, author of *The First Time Is Best: A Travel Guide to Scotland*

"Creative control! From title to cover design, from content to revision, I was in charge—like an author should be. That's what drew me to Infinity Publishing versus conventional publishing methods. The result was a great book, published at an affordable cost and in a reasonable amount of time!"

- Eddie L. Phelts, author of *Let Me Call You Sweethearts*

"Thank you so much for creating the most beautiful book on planet Earth. You guys deserve a round of applause ten times over. When I first received my book, it had a beautiful cover and layout. You went beyond my expectations. I am honored to be an Infinity author. This is truly the greatest moment of my life. There is nothing else in the world that can compare to being a published author. You guys were patient with the process and easy to talk to. I never thought in my life that I could complete this book. Not only was the production of the book professional, it was well put together. My friends and family were amazed. I would highly recommend your company to anyone that is looking to publish. All that I can say is: Wow!! Amazing!! I especially love my cover. I couldn't ask for more professionalism. It was phenomenal!!"

- Stephen Piperno, author of *Is Life Worth It?*

From Industry Professionals

"I have been working with Infinity Publishing for over a year and I find working with them very professional. As a pioneer in POD book publishing, they have helped pave the way for the rest of us to participate in this now expanding segment of publishing. We are looking forward to working with Infinity to provide their authors additional services and exposure to the publishing trade through our PW Select Program."

- Cevin Bryerman, *Publishers Weekly*

"Several years ago I toured Infinity's physical operation and was impressed by its commitment to quality and its hands-on approach with authors. You won't just be a number here."

- Mark Levine, author of *The Fine Print of Self-Publishing*

(*Mark Levine's book* The Fine Print of Self-Publishing *analyzes the contracts and services of 45 companies.*)

"Infinity Publishing, the way to see your book in print. Professionally packaged, fairly priced, your first step to a best-seller."

- Helen Wolf, Writing Events Program Chair, Pearl S. Buck International

"Infinity Publishing is the new age of publishing. For an author looking to take control of their work and self-publish, Infinity should always be a consideration. The Infinity team has the strength of a solid traditional publishing background that you won't find with the 'big' self-publishing giants. Every author receives the personalized consideration they need no matter if it is their first book or their tenth. Infinity works along with each author as they help bring their book to life. They are the future of boutique self-publishing."

-     Penny Sansevieri, CEO, Author Marketing Experts, Inc.
       and author of *Red Hot Internet Marketing*

"I have been a speaker at the Infinity conferences for several years, and each has been more rewarding and challenging than the last. The first-time attendees always bring an open mind and demanding inquisitiveness that forces me to prepare new and updated material to present. The returning attendees seem to have learned from the previous conferences and have applied their newfound knowledge. Their questions reflect that experience, and their willingness to help me help the 'newbies' is gratifying. The Infinity conferences always bring out the best in the speakers and attendees for the satisfaction and education of all."

–   Brian Jud, author of *How to Make Real Money Selling Books*
       and *Beyond the Bookstore*

Part 8

PUBLISHING OPTIONS & SERVICES

Our Publishing Options

Infinity makes it easy to publish by taking care of all of the pre-publishing formalities. We will expertly format your book's interior in a style that you'll love. Our art department will create premium-level cover artwork unique to your book. We offer a wide range of copy editing and marketing options for you to choose from. You may even publish your book online with our one-step Authors Concierge service and save 10%. We make the hard stuff simple. See all of our standard features on the web at www.infinitypublishing.com/remarkables.

All-Inclusive Publishing Packages

Classic American authors are the inspiration for Infinity Publishing's publishing programs. Once unknowns like Henry David Thoreau, Louisa May Alcott, Edgar Allen Poe and Mark Twain were at one time, all new authors, starting out on their own publishing journey. Authors have even more opportunities to make their way from writer to published author when they partner with Infinity Publishing. We want every author to have a classic publishing experience; from production, to distribution and marketing. We are looking for definitive talent. The next generation of authors, that will be a future masterwork. Let our team of publishing professionals work with you to publish your title. We offer premier publishing services and our publishing packages provide more value than you'll find anywhere else. Our authors deserve the very best.

Will your book be the next Infinity Publishing classic?

Thoreau $1,499

> *A truly good book teaches me better than to read it. I must soon lay it down, and commence living on its hint. What I began by reading, I must finish by acting.* ~Henry David Thoreau

Best known for his book *Walden*, Thoreau was an American author and poet. A writer who used nature as his inspiration. Whatever your inspiration may be, we hope our simplest of publishing package options would be just what Thoreau would have chosen. The basic necessities to get your book published, without the frills. This publishing program is available for any genre and is recommended for authors writing personal family memories or for an author, looking to publish a good quality book at a bargain price-point.

It contains all of the items for our original SBW (softcover Black & White interior book) package plus the following add-ons: eBook conversion, extended distribution, Library of Congress and US Copyright registration, 5 Free Books (shipped with the first Author book order), Half Hour Marketing Consultation (comprised of 2 - 15 minute consultations plus a personalized marketing plan) plus Publicity Marketing Materials consisting of 250 units each of Postcards, Bookmarks, Business Cards and Sell Sheet and 10 Posters.

Alcott $3,199

Good books, like good friends, are few and chosen; the more select, the more enjoyable. ~Louisa May Alcott

Louisa May Alcott wrote her beloved classic novel, *Little Women*, in 1868. Her strong ties too family, is one of the elements that draws readers into her work. At Infinity Publishing, we feel just as strongly about our family of authors. Our Alcott publishing package is designed with the novelist in mind. It has all of the basics and with more marketing and book promotional exposure. Ideal for any author looking for a well-rounded publishing and marketing program. We know Ms. Alcott would approve.

The Alcott includes everything that the Thoreau Package includes except that the it starts with our original HBW package (Hardcover Black & White interior book) plus the following add-ons: 10 Free Books are included with this package (author can choose the type of books with a maximum cover price value of $500.00 and the free books will be shipped with the Author's first book order of 50 units of the same type), One Hour Marketing Consultation (instead of the Half Hour), Manuscript Evaluation, Contemporary Publicity Marketing Materials Kit (includes Website Design, Digital Postcard, Electronic Sell Sheet and Press Release write-up), Online Distribution of the Press Release to 250 recipients over the various newswire services (including PR Log, PR Web, etc.).

Poe $4,599

Deep into that darkness peering, long I stood there, wondering, fearing, doubting, dreaming dreams no mortal ever dared to dream before. ~ Edgar Allan Poe

Edgar Allan Poe was a writer that defined his genre, taking it to another level. Using imagery of the dark and disturbed, his work draws readers in, creating fear and excitement all in the same breath. His stories linger in the mind even after the book has been closed. Think back to his incredible short story, *The Tell-tale Heart* and you can probably hear the sound of the heart beating. It's something you never forget. When the time comes for you to publish your unforgettable work, we should consider our Edgar Allan Poe Publishing Package. He is impressive and an American classic author you hate to love, simply because his work keeps you up at night.

The Poe package provides the author with the option to print his book in any of the formats that we have available, i.e. in both hardcover and softcover interior, but has the option to choose either full color or black & white interior. It includes everything that the Alcott offers plus the following add-ons: 15 Free Books (author can choose the type of books for a maximum cover price value of $750.00 and the free books will be shipped with the Author's first book order of 50 units of the same type), Online distribution of the Press Release to 500 recipients over the various newswire services (instead of 250) plus, Basic Editorial Copyediting services up to 35,000 words (this includes all material submitted, including Author Bio and Synopsys (additional number of words will be billed at the current rate per word), $100 towards a Book Fair of the Author's choice (although the author has the option to choose from any of our available list of Book Fair Services, this coupon must be redeemed within 6 months from the date of purchase of the all-inclusive publishing package).

Twain $5,199

We write frankly and fearlessly but then we "modify" before we print. ~Mark Twain

Mark Twain was tenacious with a pen and he wasn't afraid to speak his mind. His books The Adventures of Tom Sawyer and its sequel, Adventures of Huckleberry Finn helped define him as a great American writer. He was also a speaker and innovator, and his speeches are still studied today. For independent authors on their own persistent paths to publishing greatness, we recommend our Twain publishing package. Publishing, marketing and more – this package will take your title down your own right path. Work along with an Infinity Publishing professional every step of your journey. His books are classics for any business leader, big or small. As a tribute to this American icon, we celebrate authors and speakers with platforms to build and grow.

This all-inclusive publishing package includes everything that the Poe includes plus the following add-ons: 20 Free Books (author can choose the type of books for a maximum cover price of

$1,000.00 and the free books will be shipped with the Author's first book order of 100 units of the same type), Online distribution of the Press Release to 1,000 recipients over the various newswire services (instead of 500), Book Evaluation Service for Books in Distribution, plus the Book2Look Service.

The following chart provides you with a quick overview of what is included in each of the above packages.

All-inclusive Publishing Packages

Package Benefits Include	Thoreau	Alcott	Poe	Twain
Author Advocate and Author Representative assigned to Author	✓	✓	✓	✓
Hard Cover and/or Soft Cover Options*	Softcover	Hardcover	Hardcover	Hardcover
eBook Conversion	✓	✓	✓	✓
US Based phone and e-mail support	✓	✓	✓	✓
Unlimited number of images	✓	✓	✓	✓
Custom Book Cover Design	✓	✓	✓	✓
ISBN	✓	✓	✓	✓
Author retains copyright	✓	✓	✓	✓
Proof Books for author review (print books only)	✓	✓	✓	✓
40 corrections included (not including images)	✓	✓	✓	✓
Global Distribution (Amazon, B&N and BBOTW.COM, etc.)	✓	✓	✓	✓
Books-InPrint Listing	✓	✓	✓	✓
Extended Distribution Program Listing	✓	✓	✓	✓
Bookstore Return Policy	✓	✓	✓	✓
Online Storefront at BBOTW.com	✓	✓	✓	✓
Author pricing discounts on Books	✓	✓	✓	✓
Monthly Royalty Payments	✓	✓	✓	✓
Free Review Copies	✓	✓	✓	✓
Free subscription to The Author Advocate's Newsletter	✓	✓	✓	✓
Author access to special Infinity Author marketing & promotions	✓	✓	✓	✓
Author Center online account	✓	✓	✓	✓
Library of Congress Control Number & US Copyright Registration	✓	✓	✓	✓
Publicity Marketing Materials**	✓	✓	✓	✓
Free Books***	5	10	15	20
Marketing Consultation with Personalized Marketing Plan****	✓	✓	✓	✓
Digital Postcard		✓	✓	✓
Electronic Sell Sheet		✓	✓	✓
Press Release write-up		✓	✓	✓
Website Design		✓	✓	✓
Manuscript Evaluation		✓	✓	✓
Press Release Distribution		250	500	1000
Dust Jacket (Optional)		✓	✓	✓
1-Hour Audio Book			✓	✓
Editorial Services - Basic Copyediting up to 35,000 words			✓	✓
$100 towards a Book Fair Service*****			✓	✓
Book Evaluation for Books in Distribution				✓
Book2Look Service				✓
Package List Price	*$1,499*	*$3,199*	*$4,599*	*$5,199*

*　　The Alcott, Poe and Twain Packages include both the Hard Cover and Soft Cover versions of the book; Poe and Twain include full color interior option

**　　Publicity Marketing Materials include 250 units each of Postcards, Bookmarks, Business Cards and Sell Sheets plus 10 Posters

***　　Free Books will be of the higher valued book version (at a maximum cover price of $50.00) and will be shipped with the first order placed by the Author

****　　The Thoreau Package comes with a Half hour Marketing Consultation, while Alcott, Poe and Twain Packages include a One hour Marketing Consultation

*****　　$100 coupon towards a Book Fair Services must be redeemed within 6 months of purchase.

A-La-Carte Publishing Packages

For those authors who are not looking for the All-inclusive packages, they still have the option to purchase one of our A-la-carte publishing packages.

Softcover Packages

Softcover B&W Interior (SBW)　　　　　　$599

Softcover, full-color cover, black-and-white interior, includes a premium custom cover design*, advanced interior formatting*, ISBN, unlimited interior images, hardcopy galley proof*, returnability for stores, 5 free books, standard global distribution

Softcover Color Interior (SC)　　　　　　$699

Softcover, full-color cover, color interior, includes a premium custom cover design*, advanced interior formatting*, ISBN, unlimited interior images, hardcopy galley proof*, returnability for stores, 5 free books, standard global distribution

Hardcover Packages

Hardcover B&W Interior (HBW)　　　　　　$849

Full-color hardcover, black-and-white interior, includes a premium custom cover design*, advanced interior formatting*, ISBN, unlimited interior images, hardcopy galley proof*, returnability for stores, black-and-white interior, dust jacket (optional), eBook publishing, and 10 free books (5 hardcover, 5 softcover).

Hardcover Color Interior (HC)　　　　　　$949

Full-color hardcover, with color interior, includes a premium custom cover design*, advanced interior formatting*, ISBN, unlimited interior images, hardcopy galley proof*, returnability for stores, color interior, dust jacket (optional), eBook publishing, and 10 free books (5 hardcover, 5 softcover).

Other companies charge extra for hardcopy galleys and what they deem as "premium" cover design and "advanced" interior formatting. All of our books are custom created with no hidden fees or extra charges.

eBooks

eBook Design and Conversion (eB) $349
includes premium formatting, color cover and interior-page creation, and all of our major online distribution channels, including iPad, Kindle, Nook, and more.

eBook Conversion (eBC) $199
add to your SBW or SC packages or for books that are currently published by Infinity Publishing and do not require additional design or formatting, includes all of our major online distribution channels.

Audio Books

The 1-Hour Audio™ Book (1HA) $599
Publish streamlined nonfiction, fiction short stories, children's, or poetry books of approximately 11,000 words for 1-hour of audio. Published as a single CD product and is distributed via the iTunes Store, Audible.com, and many others.

Unabridged Audio Books (AB)   Call for quote
The ultimate in professional presentation. Books are recorded in specially designed recording studios with a director and engineer on each session. Every second of audio is edited where mouth clicks, swirls, and other noises are replaced with clean room sound. These books will be made available where Audio Books are sold.

Enhancements and Other Services
Included in all our print and eBook publishing formats are advanced interior formatting, unlimited images, a premium-level custom full-color cover (front and back), ISBN, and comprehensive distribution. Also included with all publishing options is help via an Author Advocate who will work with you every step of the way, from your first inquiry to your first book signing. Below, you will find descriptions of production, distribution, and editorial and marketing services that you may utilize to enhance the quality and performance of your promotional efforts.

Production Services

Scanning and embedding photos/illustrations   **$10 per scan**

Resizing and embedding photos/illustrations   **$5 per scan**

LCCN (Library of Congress Control Number) & US Copyright
Registration   **$150 per title**

Advance Reading Copies (ARC)   **$275**

Utilizing Advance Reading Copies is an essential part of many book-marketing plans. This program enables Infinity authors to send out Advance Reading Copies (ARCs) to specific reviewers and columnists who might be interested or who have expressed an interest to the author in receiving his or her book before it becomes available for sale.

Before receiving their proof books from Infinity, authors have the option of enrolling in our Advance Reading Copies program. When authors receive their regular proof copies, they will also receive 24 books with ADVANCE READING COPY printed boldly across the front and back covers. Infinity will also provide 24 book mailers, 24 mailing labels with Infinity's return address, and 24 announcement cards explaining that the complimentary ARC is provided per the recipient's prior correspondence with the author. These 24 ARCs do not count as the author's first book order. (Books are provided in full color soft cover format and additional charges may apply for color interior books)

While the author's book moves through production, the author has time to compile a list of individuals to contact and offer an ARC as soon as it is available. When these contacts agree to accept an ARC book, the author must be sure to mail it and follow up with the reviewer.

If you're the author of a nonfiction special-interest niche book, contact the top experts in that specialized field of interest—they'll often mention your book as a fresh insight into the topic and perhaps write an endorsing blurb you can use when promoting your book. Novelists can use ARCs to send to reading circles that are known for their interest in the author's genre.

CD in a Book™ $200 setup plus $5 extra per book
While writing your book, did you ever wish that there was another way for you to help readers experience your imagery or implement your ideas? Since we now produce audio books in-house (through Spoken Books Publishing), we now offer our authors the opportunity to attach a CD to the inside back cover of their books in a tamperproof sleeve.

There are many ways a CD can enhance a printed book. Poets can give voice to their poems by including a CD with a selection of poetry—hearing a poet's inflection brings a new meaning to their words. Travel narratives could be accompanied by full-color photographs, or even samples of a city's sounds. Books with references to databases of contact information, worksheets, and PDF forms could include a CD filled with a variety of different kinds of computer-friendly and printer-ready files. Historical novelists could show the dress of the period, military uniforms, and weapons of the era—history can come alive with the digital sparkles of a slide show. The possibilities for supplemental material that can be recorded on a CD are vast and will ultimately increase the value of your printed book.

Distribution Services
At Infinity Publishing we provide the most extensive distribution network opportunities available to independent authors. Distribution is a key component to marketing any title and we want to enhance every author's success with the industry leading, distribution partners. Infinity Publishing holds the resources to distribute your Print, eBook, and Audio book to a worldwide audience of readers.

Global Distribution for Print and eBooks $FREE
All Infinity Publishing authors publishing in print receive our Global Distribution Service option which is a standard component in all of our publishing packages. This service includes distribution to Amazon.com and BarnesandNoble.com. Additionally, each book will be made available for order by bookstores and libraries via our partner Baker & Taylor, the world's largest distributor of physical and digital content. As a BONUS, every book is listed and available for purchase at Infinity

Publishing's own online bookstore, Buy Books on the Web (www.bbotw.com). All eBook titles will be available to Sony, Blio, Overdrive, and Amazon.

Extended Distribution $199

If you're looking to expand your book's reach, our powerful Extended Distribution service will make your softcover black and white interior book available through one of the largest book distributors in the world: Lightning Source (Ingram Book Company's printing division). This Extended Distribution Service provides even more exposure for your title, making it available to be purchased worldwide by over 10,000 libraries and over 50,000 bookstores.

Essential Editorial Services

Essential Editorial Services helps to improve the fundamentals of your book and includes an editorial evaluation and one of three possible levels of copyediting: Basic, Substantive, or Premium. The recommended level of editing will depend upon the time required to properly edit your book. Your experienced copyeditor will go line-by-line, correcting errors in grammar and punctuation, highlighting passages that need improvement, and addressing problem areas in phrasing and word choice. If your manuscript requires it, your editor will make minor structural changes to improve flow, clarity, and readability.

Manuscript Evaluation $179

The Infinity Manuscript Evaluation is the cornerstone of our Essential Editorial Services. This is the first step towards determining the level of editing required for your book—honest feedback from a seasoned editor. You'll receive a comprehensive 10- to 12-page evaluation report and a 4- to 5-page sample edit. One of the following levels of editing will be recommended.

Basic Copyediting $0.019 per word ($150 min.)

This service is appropriate for manuscripts that require attention to basic writing mechanics. Your editor will work through the entire text, correcting errors in spelling, grammar, and punctuation as well as minor errors in syntax and word choice.

Substantive Copyediting $0.025 per word

Some manuscripts require a higher level of editorial attention than basic copyediting provides. In addition to correcting spelling, punctuation and grammar, your editor will make specific recommendations to clarify meaning, promote consistency, and smooth the flow of the text.

Premium Copyediting $0.032 per word

This service is recommended for manuscripts that need extensive structural and organizational work at the word, sentence, and paragraph levels. In addition to addressing mechanics, your editor will make recommendations to improve the manuscript's overall composition and strengthen technical elements in the writing. This service is an ideal choice for non-native English speakers and some first-time authors.

PLEASE NOTE:

- Occasionally, the amount of editorial service required to edit a manuscript to industry standard may fall outside the scope of the above services. In those rare instances, a separate quote will be provided.

- Total time for copyediting: 2 to 4 weeks

Advanced Editorial Services

Infinity's Advanced Editorial Services help you develop your concept or complete your book and give you the opportunity to work with experienced editors and writing coaches who are among the best in the industry. Even if you haven't committed one word to the page, your Book Genesis writing coach will help you develop your manuscript, from concept to execution. If you've already begun writing, we also offer individualized developmental editing and coaching to help you complete the manuscript you've started.

Are you struggling to complete your manuscript? Would you like to get it done in months rather than years? Do you have a concept for a book but haven't written a single word? Let one of our professional editors or writing coaches guide you across the finish line.

Hourly Development and Coaching

A flexible, individualized program that gives you the help you need from a Book Genesis editor on an hourly basis. This is a great choice for authors who may already have a first draft or partial manuscript but need professional help to complete their book. A five-hour minimum start-up purchase is required; additional developmental editing and coaching services may be purchased in two-hour increments at the rate of $150/hour.

Book Marketing Services

Once your book is published, you'll need help with marketing. Personalized support from your own personal Author Advocate comes standard, helping you formulate marketing plans that will help sell your book. We also offer a range of professionally designed and printed promotional materials, as well as leading-edge online marketing services.

There is no sense of satisfaction greater than publishing your book. But once your book is on the market, how will people know how to buy it? Nowhere else can you find the level of support provided by Infinity. Your Author's Advocate will provide marketing help by way of the vast experience we've accumulated over 14 years of being in the business. We have a range of optional, professionally designed and printed promotional materials. Choose the size that fits your promotional efforts.

The Value of Book Marketing

The two most important factors in the sale of a book are good word-of-mouth and a solid marketing approach. We help take care of the good word-of-mouth by providing buyers with a beautiful product delivered quickly. We also help your marketing efforts by offering our marketing packages, consultation, newsletters, and conferences. As a published author, you will let people know about your book's value to them and that it's available for sale. This essentially is what marketing is all about.

Credibility Is King

In an effort to attract authors, some publishers offer to blindly send hundreds of press releases to many different media outlets. This is referred to in the industry as "media spamming," meaning that the media outlets receive hundreds of press releases from those publishers daily.

Bulk releases have little credibility and are seen as an annoyance by the media, not as a source of reliable information. Bulk press-release programs seem to exist for the sake of inflating the publishing setup fees paid by the author. At Infinity, we don't do that. A properly executed marketing plan involving press releases requires a different approach. Press releases need to be sent judiciously to targeted media and written with a personal touch. There are many books on the subject and there are many publicists available to you who can perform this task the right way, which will be a better value for you and give you a better chance of gaining tangible results.

Publicity Marketing Materials

Marketing is one of the differentiators that can turn your book into a highly successful one. To support all of your marketing efforts we offer Infinity Authors a range of professionally designed publicity marketing kits with full color products printed on high quality UV coated cardstock materials. Choose from 3 kits with 2 design options – horizontal or vertical layouts. Click here to see the design options. Included is a choice of our Digital Publicity Marketing Kit to provide the Infinity Author with all of the tools to digitally market their book.

Publicity Marketing Kits available in 3 options with 2 designs to choose from:

Renaissance $595
Our Renaissance publicity marketing kit includes 250 Business Cards, 250 Bookmarks. 250 Postcards, 250 Sell Sheets, 10 Posters, 25 copies of the Author's Book (in softcover black & white interior with price upgrade for color and hardcover formats) and Marketing Book – Grassroots Marketing for Authors and Publishers valued at $24.95

Modern $925
Our Modern publicity marketing kit includes 500 Business Cards, 500 Bookmarks, 500 Postcards, 500 Sell Sheets, 25 Posters, 50 copies of the Author's Book (in softcover black & white interior

with price upgrade for color and hardcover formats) and Marketing Book – Grassroots Marketing for Authors and Publishers valued at $24.95

Contemporary $975

Our Contemporary publicity marketing kit includes Digital Postcard, Electronic Sell Sheet, Press release write-up, Website Design

If you have already ordered one of our Publicity Marketing Kits are now you to replenish one or more items we offer our Infinity Authors the possibility to order one or more of the following.

- 250 Business Cards $149
- 250 Bookmarks $149
- 250 Postcards $199
- 10 Posters $149
- 250 Sell Sheets $199

Marketing Services

Marketing Consultation Service $495

Marketing is the driving force behind book sales. As a new author, or even a veteran writer, having a professional book marketing expert work with you to coordinate your marketing plan is a must. Infinity Publishing offers a one-on-one marketing consultation service that will leave the author with a customized marketing plan to suit the needs of each author's goals, budget and marketing objectives.

The Marketing Consultation Service & Personalized Marketing Plan includes: 2 – 30 minute consultations, 30 Day Marketing Calendar, Personalized Marketing Plan reviewed with our in-house Marketing Expert during the second 30 minute consultation, Guest Blogging Invite, plus a Free Marketing Guide eBook. My Book's Published...Now What??? will be yours to enjoy.

Website Design $499

A custom website is a must for authors in today's world of publishing. Some authors need a book-focused website. Others would benefit from an author-oriented site. Our personalized services and one-on-one guidance will lead you through the process of developing a website that can help you achieve your personal goals. Our website packages start at $499 and include design services, self-updatable pages, a blog tool, web traffic reports, and more.

Other Marketing Service Options

Infinity Publishing offers a wide variety of marketing and promotional services, including online marketing and promotion, social media campaigns and support, blogging programs, book fairs, book reviews, promotional events and more. Every book is unique and we don't assume to know the marketing goals of every author, so we prefer to customize our marketing services for each and every author. We do offer several marketing services that can be purchased a-la-carte. We highly recommend that authors first invest in our marketing consultation service, which provides a personalized plan with additional recommendations.

Book2Look Widget $395

A truly innovative book marketing tool, Book2Look widgets are easy to use and a powerful digital boost to any title. Authors control their marketing via this incredible online widget. Your book's information is uploaded and instantly your Book2Look widget is ready to use right away.

Book2Look includes: Book Reviews, Shares sample chapters, Book cover images, Author interviews, Book video trailers as well as Social media and just about any other media to promote your book.

Update as often as needed. If you want to spread the word about your book and increase sales, Book2Look is an excellent and cost-effective solution.

Book Review Service $150

This service is available for books that meet certain requirements. The books must have been professionally edited, no exceptions. Books must also have had professional book cover and interior formatting design. Book marketing consultation along with marketing plan is required for books to be reviewed for consideration for bookstore and specialty sales channel distribution options. Following the review, the author will be provided a summary of recommendations for the book's potential for wider distribution.

Publicity Marketing Services

At Infinity we believe that every book's success is based on a targeted Marketing Campaign supported by a Publicity Campaign that helps the Author create awareness not only of the book and its content but also, and most of the time, more importantly, about the Authors and your story.

Thousands of books are published each month in different formats and the battle for media attention is more competitive than ever. With this in mind we have created Publicity Campaigns that include both traditional and online campaigns unique to the Book Genre and Author and led by a professional book publicist ready to work with Infinity's Authors to assist their books become best sellers. There are a number of Campaigns to choose from, but the Kick-start Media Campaign helps you lead the way. To learn more about our Publicity Marketing Services contact any of our Author Advocates and they will provide you with additional information on our packages.

Book Publicity Kick-start Media Campaign $1,999

This service is designed for a quick, highly targeted media outreach by a professional book publicist, with you, the author, following up and scheduling all opportunities. Your publicist will create a press release for your approval and "pitch" targeted media to local, regional and national print (magazine and newspaper), broadcast (radio and television), and online (e-zines, blogs, websites) outlets across the U.S. and Canada. Your publicist will also create a high priority media list of 20 contacts and will mail them your book and press release.

At the end of the three week campaign, your publicist will guide you on how to continue follow up activities to encourage media coverage. You will receive information on all media contacts that expressed interest in your book and a publicity manual with tips to promote yourself and your book.

Charitable Causes

ECO-LIBRIS "100 TREE PROJECT" $50
– Trees (100) are planted in the name of your book.

Closing Notes

We have published more than 6,000 titles since 1997. We offer the fastest turnaround, the best service, and the most freedom and value of any publisher hands down.

We are here to help writers achieve their goals as published authors. By following the instructions in this book, you will be able to quickly prepare your work, submit it to us, and, as a published author, reap the benefits of being alive in the age of information.

Having a published book will provide you with something tangible on which to focus your promotional efforts. Before you know it, your beautifully prepared book will be in the appreciative hands of your readers. Your book, made available worldwide, can be the vehicle for your writing success.

Many have endured a tough time out there—dealing with numerous rejections, difficult agents, apathetic publishers, pushy editors, and fast-talking scammers. We know what it is like to be rejected, but we understand that many greats have come before us who were also rejected many times before being recognized. Heck, even the Beatles were rejected!

We hope that you haven't lost sight of what your goals are and what ultimately fuels your soul. If you are a writer who has authored a book worthy of publishing and you want an easy and inexpensive way to connect with the masses, then we are the right publisher for you.

We invite you to take the next step with us. If you and your book are ready, a whole world of opportunity is waiting to be tapped into. In the meantime, if you have any questions, feel free to contact us toll-free at 877-BUY-BOOK (877-289-2665) or by e-mail at *info@infinitypublishing.com.*

Good luck and good writing!

Infinity Publishing

Part 9

FREQUENTLY ASKED QUESTIONS

What must I send for you to publish my book?

1) a signed and completed publishing agreement; 2) a floppy disk, CD, or USB flash drive containing a digital file of your book and supporting documents (blurb, bio, etc.); 3) the required payment for setup. Under certain circumstances, we can accept a hard copy in lieu of a digital file on disk. For the easiest submission method, use our free online Authors Concierge™ service located on our website.

Besides the digital file of my book, what else do I need to prepare for you?

We require that you also provide us with descriptive content for our website. For example, we need a 100-word description of your book and a 100-word bio about you. These are comparable to what you would find on the inside of a hardback book sleeve or the back cover of a paperback book. We also require a 1,000-word-maximum excerpt from the book. This will be used as a "sneak peek" which consumers will be able to read to see the quality of your writing. The final thing we need is a 30-word blurb.

What is a blurb?

The 30-word blurb is simply a brief description of your book. Don't go crazy trying to create this content. Being simple and to the point works best, using key words and phrases to draw your audience in. Just ask yourself, "What is this book about, bottom line?"

How do I prepare the digital file of my book?

Follow our guidelines in part 3 of this book. Go as far as you can to prepare your work, send it in to us with the Publishing Agreement and payment, and we will fix it up and take it the rest of the way.

I am trying to format my book to your specifications. I would like to call you and ask about formatting my digital file. Is that a good way to do it?

No. Because it is difficult to answer formatting questions over the phone, we ask that you instead just go as far as you can and submit your digital file to us as-is. This will not affect the quality of your proof book. We do a lot of fine-tuning to book files regardless of how much preparation went into them by the author.

I can't get the page numbers to work.

Don't worry about it. Send us your work to be published and we will number the pages for you.

Should I type the page numbers on each page?

You should never manually hand-type page numbers. If you cannot figure it out, leave them out altogether and we'll insert them. Just give us clear instructions on where page number one starts.

Can my book have any color for the interior other than black or grayscale?

Yes, although most of our book interiors are printed in high-quality black and white, we also offer full-color softcover and hardbound books of all sizes. Of course, our book covers are printed in full color and are always laminated.

Your publishing agreement says a work, if fiction, must not be based on real events or places. So does that mean that you will not publish historical fiction?

No. What you must not do in a fictional work is use real people or their likenesses. Everyone has the right to prohibit their usage in a book sold on the market commercially. Obviously, all fiction is based on reality in some way. What you must do is take the names and characteristics of any characters in your book and change them so much that they are not recognizable. For a work of historical fiction, if the characters are famous and are from more than fifty years ago, it should be okay.

What if I want to use nonstandard fonts in my book?

If you are using non-standard fonts please make sure that they are included with your submission files. If you need further information or assistance please contact us at 1-877-289-2665.

In what formats do you accept submissions?

We accept Microsoft Word, Corel WordPerfect, AppleWorks, and Adobe PDF files for book interiors. If the interior of your book is created on InDesign, PageMaker, or Quark, then you must create a PDF; we do not accept these formats for book interiors in their native format. Book-cover artwork can be provided on the same disk as everything else as JPEGs, TIFFs, a PDF, or as files in Quark, PageMaker, or Photoshop format with PC versions of fonts provided.

Do you accept work created on an Apple Macintosh computer?

Absolutely. Use Microsoft Word or AppleWorks. If you used Quark, Adobe Illustrator, InDesign, or PageMaker, then convert the book's interior file to a PDF. Make your PDF with no compression, start with 300-dpi images in your original file, and embed every font used.

Can my book be available through the Ingram distribution system?

Yes. If you order our optional Extended Distribution Package ($199), we will submit your softcover black and white interior book into their system.

How do I determine the price of the book?

The size and number of pages determine our suggested list price. See the How Our Books Are Priced section in this book for pricing.

Can I include photos in my book?

Yes. We'll scan your photos and illustrations for $10 each. If you have access to a good scanner, scan them and save them as 200 dpi JPEGs or TIFFs and embed them in your book file. There is **no extra charge for photos scanned and inserted into the file by the author.** Remember, all interior photos are printed in high quality black and white only unless you choose the color option.

When will my book be ready for sale?

If the materials you submit are complete, your book can be available for sale in two to three months. You'll see your first actual proof book in about eight to ten weeks after you submit your work. We recommend you take at least a week to proofread the book. We take about two weeks to make corrections. Most books will require a second proof book.

What types of books do you accept?

From poetry to pet grooming, we accept all types of books! We do reserve the right to reject books at any time for any reason. Please be aware that we will not accept books that are grossly offensive, potentially libelous, or illegal in nature. It is all right to publish an autobiography that talks about abuse in your childhood, but if a court has not found the abuser guilty of that criminal action, you must mask their identity to avoid libel. If your book resembles anything that could be considered dangerous to society (i.e. "how to build a bomb"), we will not publish it.

How do I handle book signings?

Our books are returnable by bookstores. However, when you are planning a book signing, it is still best for you to bring the books yourself. This is the easiest way to guarantee the quantity of books available at the event, and will also translate into a hassle-free experience for the hosting bookstore.

When and how do I get paid?

Each month, we will send you a royalty statement with an accompanying check (when applicable). All monetary transactions are in U.S. dollars only. There is a two-month grace period from the sale to the creation of the royalty payment. For instance, checks for January sales made directly through Infinity are printed in March. Sales that occur between bookstores and their customers may take longer to appear on your royalty statement. Checks are only printed if the amount owed is more than $20. Royalties continue to accrue until the amount owed exceeds this amount.

What will my book look like?

Your book will be printed double-sided on high-quality, recycled white paper, with a full-color, laminated, and perfect-bound cover, just like the book in your hands! We publish books in three popular sizes: 5.5" x 8.5", 8" x 8", and 8.5" x 11". The interior will be grayscale and the cover will be full color. We also print color on the inside of the book and offer hardbound as an option.

What if I already have a book in print?

As long as you have not signed a contract that limits your ability to do so, you may submit your book to Infinity. When you publish with Infinity, you retain *all* rights to your book.

Can you edit my book?

We offer an optional in-house editorial services program that will greatly enhance your book. There is a separate contract to fill out, which you can download from our website or request by contacting us.

How much of my book will appear on your website?

In addition to the 100-word book synopsis and author's bio, you can provide an excerpt (up to 1,000 words) of your book. The front cover will also appear.

What if I already have an ISBN for my book?

A new International Standard Book Number must be issued if any of the following information is ever changed: title, publisher, content, author name, publication date, format, or binding method. We will issue an ISBN, create a barcode, and compose the copyright and disclaimer page in your book.

Will I see a copy of my book before it is listed for sale?

Yes, you will receive two or three actual copies of your book to proofread and send to the Library of Congress for copyright registration. You will approve your book before it is listed for sale.

Will my book look like it displays and prints on my computer?

Not always. Files created in word-processing programs such as Microsoft Word and Corel WordPerfect can vary when transferred from computer to computer. This is simply an aspect of digital printing.

Digital files are like children. Picture a child that behaves like an angel in front of its parent (your computer), but acts more naturally around strangers (our computers). Formatting problems that were hidden to you will reveal themselves to us. We will fix what is obvious to us, and when you get your first proof, you will point out any errors that made it into the proof. You will do this by providing us with a master list of corrections and by marking them in your proof book with a red pen.

How much will I pay for copies of my book?

For authors, the first order is 50 percent off the suggested list price. Future orders are at 40 percent off suggested list price. Any author order of 250 or more books also qualifies for the 50 percent discount. Shipping is always free for 20 or more copies; however, we do charge a handling fee of $4.50 for each ship-to address. Our website gives orders of 5 or more an automatic 40 percent discount. This is okay for authors to use, as long as their orders are for 5 or more, and for authors who have not increased the list price of the book beyond our suggested list price. Authors can always order books by calling us at 877-BUY-BOOK (877-289-2665) with a credit card number, or by mailing us a check/money order.

Do I need to copyright my book before sending it to you?

You certainly may. However, it is a common practice for the author to copyright the published version of the book. Either way, you will send the extra proof book to the Library of Congress. Minor problems with the book will not affect your protection. It is important to get the process started as soon as possible. At this time, the fee that you will pay to the Library of Congress to copyright your book is $50.

Should I put two spaces or one space between sentences? And what about justification?

For most books, we recommend that you use one space between sentences and that you justify the text. Text in poetry books is frequently right- or left-aligned or centered.

Can my book be updated after publication?

Yes. This is not like traditional printing methods where after the initial print run, you are stuck with thousands of printed books. For example, if you had written and traditionally published a book on astronomy and a new planet was discovered, the unsold books would be useless. With our method, the book could be updated for future printings, and only those books in our inventory would need to be dealt with. We charge a minimum of $100 to update a book after it has been published. We are only interested in publishing high-quality books.

How do I link my website to BBOTW.com so people can start at my website and, from there, buy my book on your website?

There is an address field in your web browser; this is the field where you ordinarily type web addresses (URLs) into. Begin by going to our site and looking up your book and clicking on it. The page shown will be the "book description page." Copy this URL and e-mail it to the person who designs your website so that he or she can make a link on your site to that page. This is the "link" to your book's page on our website. You can also use this link for marketing purposes in e-mails.

How should I prepare images that I scan myself to be inserted into my file?

When you scan your images, you should first save them as 200 dpi JPEGs. You may then insert them into your file. Cover images can be 600 dpi JPEGs, TIFFs, or BMPs.

Part 10

HOW OUR BOOKS ARE PRICED

Print Pricing

The number of pages in your book will determine the suggested list price. Be sure to include the front or unnumbered sections (such as the foreword, introduction, dedication page, table of contents, etc.) when calculating the page count.

Our suggested list prices are based on the following criteria:

❑ The book will be printed double-sided. If a book is to be printed single-sided, double the page count.

❑ While the majority of the book will be printed double-sided, there typically will be some single-sided pages in the book. Our pricing schedule takes into account three single-sided sheets per book. More than three single-sided pages in your book may lift your book into the next higher price bracket.

❑ We cannot price the book *lower* than our suggested price. We can, however, price a nonfiction book higher. With value-added pricing, you can increase the price of your book and receive 75 percent of the difference in additional royalties.

Once you have looked up your book's suggested list price, you can decide whether you would like to set the list price higher.

Color and Hardcover Book Pricing

Please speak with your Author Advocate or in-house representative to determine the best configuration and suggested list pricing.

eBook Pricing

Our eBook pricing is based on an assumption that the eBook version should be lower than the print version of your book. We look to Amazon and a few of our other retail partners in developing our pricing recommendations. We currently suggest that for the average-size eBook, you price your book within the range of $2.95 and $9.95, which, depending on the price selected, can provide a significantly higher royalty than your printed book. At Amazon, pricing your eBook above $9.95 provides a 50 percent lower royalty than if priced at $9.95 or below. We will work with each of our authors to determine best pricing.

Shipping

We charge $4.50 shipping for the first book and $1.00 for each additional book shipped. Shipping is always free for quantities of twenty books or more; however, we do charge a handling fee of $4.50 for each ship-to address.

Most shipments of two or more books are by UPS Ground, while most single-book orders are shipped by U.S. Postal Service. We can ship via UPS 3-Day, 2-Day, or Next Day for an extra charge.

We ship to Canada by first-class mail, $6.00 for the first book and $2.00 for each book thereafter. While we ship books only to the United States and Canada, our books may be purchased worldwide from Amazon.com.

Audio Book Pricing

The table below indicates the minimum price your audio book will sell for based on the CD count of your book. You can elect to set the price higher if your book warrants it. You will be paid royalties on all sales of your book. MP3 downloads will be priced on a case-by-case basis.

Maximum Word Count	<11,000	<22,000	<33,000	<44,000	<55,000	<66,000	<77,000	<88,000
CDs per audiobook	1 CD	2 CD	3 CD	4 CD	5 CD	6 CD	7 CD	8 CD
Minimum list price	9.95	12.95	15.95	17.95	19.95	21.95	24.95	27.95

Maximum Word Count	<99,000	<110,000	<121,000	<132,000	<143,000	154,000	165,000
CDs per audiobook	9 CD	10 CD	11 CD	12 CD	13 CD	14 CD	15 CD
Minimum list price	29.95	31.95	33.95	35.95	37.95	39.95	41.95

These are our standard sizes in both black & white and color interior in both softcover and hardcover:
5.5 x 8.5, 6 x 9, 8 x 8, 7 x 10, 8.5 x 11 (all sizes are in inches).

Landscape options are also available upon request.

Options for hardcover also include glossy case bound or cloth bound hardcover with a dust jacket.

In the event that your project does not fall within the sizes or options listed here, please contact us and we will be happy to provide you with special pricing or availability.

The author's first order or any author order of 250 books or more will receive a 50 percent discount. Subsequent orders receive a 40 percent discount, and will also earn a 10 percent royalty.

Contact us for information on pricing for, black & white interior, color interior and hardcover books.

Exhibit A

MEET A FEW OF OUR AUTHORS

Bob O'Connor

Historical Fiction Writer

Why did you choose INFINITY PUBLISHING?

∞

"The main thing I like about Infinity Publishing is that they do what they say they are going to do in the time period they say it will be done. I cannot find fault with that at all."

When did you know that you wanted to be a writer?

"Writing comes easy to me. I took an adult education publishing class. The teacher said there are 50 million people writing books but only about three million that were published authors. It is interesting, out of nine in that class, all who were about finished writing some kind of book, to date I am the only published author in the group."

How did you work to achieve your goals?

"I worked day and night to become published. I was driven to get that first book out and haven't stopped since."

How do you market your books?

"I seek speaking engagements with colleges, other schools, libraries, Civil War Round Tables and others. I have averaged 80-100 events each year starting in 2006 including book festivals, book stores, grocery stores, and senior centers. I work every day to reach out and make myself available to speak."

Leonard Renier

Finance

Writer

Why did you choose INFINITY PUBLISHING?

∞

"I researched many other publishers, and Infinity made the most sense. Once I started working with them, I found that they're a great group of people serious about my success."

When did you first start writing?

"I have owned my own business since I was 21-years-old and worked in the financial services business for over 30 years. 12 years ago, I was speaking publicly and discovered I could make people laugh, cry, and introduce concepts and ideas in an entertaining fashion. I founded the Wealth and Wisdom Institute and organization of professionals from across the country dedicated to informing and educating the public regarding the follies of traditional financial thinking. I first started writing because I continued to grow increasingly frustrated with the financial services business where it was all about profit."

What has publishing done for you?

"Publishing opened a new door for my business."

What advice do you have for other writers and authors in terms of publishing and marketing their books?

"Marketing and promotion is a daily event. Getting in front of people is the key – also getting endorsements. I'm not sure, but we've sold about 40,000 books with no marketing, only word of mouth."

Jennifer Monahan

Non-fiction Travel Writer

Why did you choose INFINITY PUBLISHING?

∞

"I researched many other publishers, and Infinity made the most sense. Once I started working with them, I found that they're a great group of people serious about my success."

When did you know that you wanted to be a writer?

"I traveled throughout my life and I would write letters home from wherever I was living or vacationing. I didn't realize it, but I was a travel writer early on."

What has publishing done for you?

"Publishing my book has given me a new career. Being an author opens doors where there were no doors before."

How did you work to achieve your goals?

"In 2001, I took a seminar that caused me to reflect on what I wanted as a child. I recalled my dream of writing. I had spent two months traveling across Australia and kept a journal of my time there. I finally took the journal out of the closet and started writing. Two-and-a-half years later, Infinity published it."

Laura Sepesi

Fantasy Writer

Why did you choose INFINITY PUBLISHING?

∞

"I chose Infinity Publishing because of their professionalism, commitment to quality, and attentiveness to their authors. I was lucky enough to win contracts to publish my first two books with them. I highly recommend them to every author actively working to get his or her book out into the marketplace."

When did you know that you wanted to be a writer?

"I had a passion for storytelling from an early age. I began drafting my first novel the summer after I finished high school and continued to work on it while attending college full time."

What has publishing done for you?

"It has given me the chance to share my stories with readers all over the world. Being a published author is an amazing experience, and has opened the doors to many exciting opportunities for my work and my professional career. I love being able to tell people that I'm a published author."

What advice do you have for other writers and authors in terms of publishing and marketing their books?

"Take the initiative to get your book published and out into the marketplace. You are the greatest promoter of your book, so invest the time, money, and energy into creating the best product possible. Once you have that book, get it out into the world."

Terrence Shulman

Non-fiction
Writer

Why did you choose INFINITY PUBLISHING?

∞

"I can say that I've always been satisfied with Infinity from the get-go when I worked with them and published my first book with them in 2003. They were reasonably priced and believed in me and coached me through the process very well."

When did you know that you wanted to be a writer?

"My parents divorced when I was 10 and I found some outlets through writing songs and poetry. However, at the age of 14, I also began shoplifting. I was arrested when I was 21, but got a slap on the wrist. When I graduated college, I entered law school. Then my father died and I started shoplifting again. I was arrested for a second time and finally came out to my family about my habit. Just before graduating in 1997 I had the idea for a book about shoplifting addiction based on my story and the stories I'd heard from various members of my support group I started."

What has publishing done for you?

"It has helped so many and has been a calling card for me to be recognized as an expert for both clients seeking counseling as well as for media interview—including my appearance on Oprah in late 2004! Oprah became the launching pad to start my own business---The Shulman Center for Compulsive Theft & Spending—in 2004."

Exhibit B

CUSTOM
BOOK COVERS